Clamps, Whiskey, and A Scarf

LAVISHLY LOST

IN A LOVELY LIBRARIAN

STEVE STONE

PAGE PUBLISHING
Conneaut Lake, PA

First originally published by Page Publishing 2022

ISBN 978-1-6624-7839-0 (pbk)
ISBN 978-1-6624-7840-6 (digital)

Printed in the United States of America

IN THE BEGINNING

Prologue

This is All for you, Loretta
I So Wish that you are able to read these words
Composed for you.
While you claimed that no one had ever
Written anything for you previously
I have never before been
So moved and so inspired
To write and create
And to simply improve myself.
Your influence will never part from me completely
I certainly had fun while I knew you
Certainly for those several months.
I Fiercely Wish I could have known you longer.
Effortlessly, even from afar,
You will continue to
Inspire me moving forward

I Fiercely Wish that I could have known you longer.
Every printed page
Every coffee Post-It note
Everything is for you

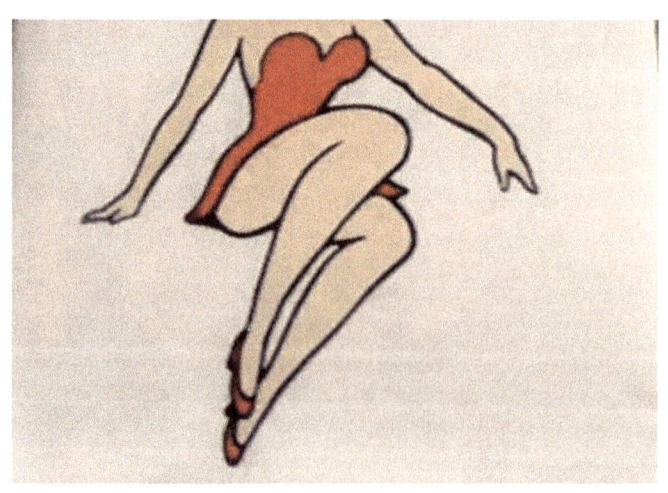

My, Oh My!

My, oh my
To my surprise
My hopeful vision is channeled
Upon a picture of unappreciated thighs

My, oh my
As fantasies certainly run high
I can merely brush and groom
My mustache disguise

My, oh my
The thoughts, the dreams, and damn the delights
Of the facial hair above my lip
Grazing and feasting between your thighs

My, oh my

GOOD MORNING
BEAUTIFUL
THE WORLD
WOULD LOVE TO LAY EYES
UPON YOUR SULTRY SMILE
TODAY

'TWAS A CLASSY PIC
INDEED DARLING

BUT REMARKABLY,
I AM NOT ALWAYS
A CLASSY DUDE

Agony

Wishes of the visual stimuli received to be followed by aroused silence
An inability to express my praise for an astounding divineness
Carnal wishes to place my lips upon her pedals,
Brush my lips up her thighs to worship in the middle.

Before shifting focus above her waist behold
Licking, smooching, sucking, biting every crease and fold
Tongue encircling each surreal areola,
Front teeth nibbling on each exquisite nipple.

Pictured enticement of black lace,
Nobly drawn upon her edible waist,
Burning Desire continues to anticipate.
Oh, my god—for goodness sake!

The Anguish of Quiet and Stillness
True challenge indeed to measure will power
For conservation of Astroglide I will vow to express myself
Cleaning and stroking ever so vigorously in my personal shower

GOOD MORNING
BEAUTIFUL
I HOPE THAT YOUR DAY
IS AS ENJOYABLE
AS YOUR
BUTT CHEEKS

8

An Oath

I promise to want you like the lion needs meat
I swear to crave your curves like the shark requires water
I vow to seek your smile like the wolf hunts for prey
I declare to dazzle your delights like the baker pounds upon dough
I marvel about your mind like the sun brightens day

I commit to keeping you satisfied as your sent pictures
Have kept me self-gratified

Happiness and confidence
I assure you

NOW THAT OUR EYES
HAVE BEEN OPENED
AS MY ZIPPER
POINTS TO THE SKY
I'VE NEVER FELT
SO ALIVE

Animalistic

You are so wickedly tempting
In every way that I have imagined
I would fantasize about someone
To be so seductively stimulating
With your provocative prowess
This intriguing engagement
Seems to be something more
Some sort of sacred want
A devilish desire of the divine
This pulsating urge
I doubt this bottomless appetite
To taste your attractive assets
Will ever be completely satisfied

I DROWNED
MYSELF IN YOUR
ALMOND EYES
WHILE MESMERIZED
BY YOUR VOICE
THIS MORNING

Aspirations

Her wine-stained lips surrounding her innocent smile
Gives me reason to strut along my path
Provides hope for an enjoyable future
Reproduces every naughty dream I've had
In beliefs that they will indeed become a reality
Whenever my sights are lucky enough to locate her
I surrender myself as property
Realizing that I belong to her
While holding aspirations
That I may call her mine

AFTER BEING STRUCK
BY THE SEDUCTIVE
SIGHT OF YOUR SULTRY
SKIN IN THE FIRST
SENT PHOTO –
THE UNQUESTIONABLE
OBJECT OF MY DESIRE
KEEPS ME SALIVATING

Somewhere

Somewhere
Behind nonfiction
Somewhere
To satisfy my new addiction
Darling on the down low
Hidden down the biography row
How we could perspire
While we are quickly fornicating
Yet so thoroughly fornicating

THE PULSE
WITHIN MY PENIS
BEATS TO YOUR
NAME

Bippity Boo!

I Like your Boobs!
Your Butt is Okay Too!

PLEASING PONDERINGS
OF YOUR POSTERIOR
PUMP PETRO
TO MY PENIS

THE BEWITCHING TRANCE
EMIT FROM YOUR
SPECTACULAR UNDERBOOB
IAAS CAST ME
UNDER A SPELL

Book's Booty

There is absolutely nothing subpar/inadequate about your posterior
My hands, nose, lips, teeth, and tongue can be entertained for hours
As you choose to place yourself above me
My delighted nose pressed against your pad
Hands upon each erogenous glute to make the laughter merrier
The youth and liveliness in your bottom begs ripe for me to devour

SULTRY SIGHTS
of YOUR
SEDUCTIVE STILL FRAMES
FIERCELY FLUSHES
FLUIDS TO MY
PHALLUS

Brave

I am anxious to share a dance with you
But my ankle is sprained and tender
Weakened from all the miles along my path
Running and jumping through obstacles
Defining and building my desire for someone like you

I will carry you to keep you warm
I will lift you up, awkwardly, if necessary
Raising as you are hindered or weighted down
Through disappointment or darkness

I think that we are both brave
To open and vividly free ourselves
As if we don't know how it can feel to be hurt
Tying and twisting while you fiercely spin me
I still cannot get enough of it

YOUR FLAWLESSLY
FINE FIGURE
FORCES A FIERCE
BLOOD FLOW
FUNNELLING TOWARD
MY PHALLUS

Breathtaking Anticipation

Your picture was Breathtaking.
You are SO Damn Beautiful, Loretta.
You have turned me into a giddy youngster,
All Excited and Chubby to receive your words.
I can't seem to get enough of you,
This thrill, this feeling, this tingling,
The saving of—
Anticipation.

Your pictured body was illuminating.
Without question, you are one of the Sexiest women I have seen.
You have created in me a Hungry lover,
So desperate and firm reaching that of the absurd,
I can't seem to want enough of you,
This urge, this longing, this yearning,
A waiting for—
Consummation.

MY TONGUE
TINGLES TENACIOUSLY
TO TASTE YOUR
TUSH.
TOTALLY.
AN UNBELIEVABLE
BITE OF BUTT

Building Stamina

Joy, Oh Joy!
Photographed underboob!
Surely sent to me to build anticipation!
No need to wonder, "Why?"

Boy, Oh Boy!
Nips for my lips and incisors too!
Sends me to build stamina via masturbation!
Quickly, I must comply.

HERE I AM
DROOLING OVER THE DRIVE
OF MY AMBITION
FALLING FASTER
INTO ECSTASY WITH
EVERY SECOND

Chances Taken

I know that you are walking
With insecurities inside you
These foolish thoughts are simply inconceivable
Because of his inexplicable actions
You feel broken and inadequate
This false belief of yours is also inconceivable

You have been trained not to express yourself
To keep your radiant beauty and arousing appeal concealed
You have been hidden, kept and caged within four walls

You should be with someone like me
You need to be cherished and understood
You should be with someone who adores being there for you
You deserve to be cared and craved for
You are entitled to be dreamed of
To star as the female in a personal-pleasure shower and fantasy

You may be afraid to step outside of these walls
Through habitual comfort and luxury
He has built around you
Free yourself of these chains he has restraining you

I want to take a chance with you
I want to have a romance with you
My pulse is quickening to set a date
Salivating heavily for the certainly savory taste

I AM NOT SURE
HOW TO TELL YOU
THAT YOU ARE
EROTICALLY TIED
TO EVERY IDEA
I HAVE EVER HAD OF
DESIRE

Demanding

Her alluring strides of confidence
Display to the world
That you can be torn to pieces
Emotionally
And still possess the stature
To demand admiration from passersby

EVER SINCE
FIRST LAYING EYES
UPON THE CURVATURE
OF YOUR BREATHTAKING
BACKSIDE
I'VE BEEN SALIVATING
TO SLIDE ALL OF MY SENSES
UP AND DOWN YOUR CRACK
ETERNALLY

Do You Think?

I don't want you to want me because I am a "nice guy"
Or because I am "so sweet" because you find my compliments flattering

I want to be the stud that you were not expecting
I want you to think that I am SSSSSSeeexxxyy!
I want to be someone who makes you breathe uneasy with passion
The guy who makes your voice heighten with startling desire
I seek to make your walk unrecognizable
With an unforeseen amount of lust in the legs of your strides
I yearn for your essence to be inexplicably yet
Infuriatingly compelled to my awkward advances

My tongue is understandably magnetized
To your every alluring curve
My taste buds vow to explore every inch
Of every crevice upon this quest

THE HEAVENLY ARCH
AND HEEL OF YOUR FOOT
HEAVIES THE HABITUAL
HARD ON ERECT
IN YOUR HONOR

REVELATION OF FLESH
ON YOUR FINE FEET
IN SANDAL FOOTWEAR
HAS FURIOUSLY FLUNG
ME INTO A
FANATIC FRENZY

Edible Pedals

Your edible pedals
Are simply incredible
The astonishing appeal of your attractive feet
Can obviously be noted as far from discreet
The appetizing grasp of your maroon toenail polish
Forcefully ignites my awakened foot fetish
Moved by the surely intentional revelation of your lower limits
Please present to me your instep for me to lick, nibble, suck, and kiss

YOU SHOVED ME
UNINTENTIONALLY
INTO AN
EROTIC ECSTASY
FROM WHICH I CAN'T
SEEM TO RECOVER

Elegance

You walked through your library doors
With such a distinguished elegance.
Delightful landscape
Hidden beneath your blouse
The taunting cuisine available
Beneath your pants.

My eyes saw you.
But Damn it, Loretta,
Did you cause my zipper
To point up sharply to the sky.

AFTER SETTING SIGHTS

ON YOUR SEDUCTIVE SKIN

I AM GROWING IMPATIENT

FOR THE DISMISSAL BELL —

ALLOWING ME TO DART HOME

AND PLEASURE MYSELF

ENTHUSIASTICALLY

Every Time

Every time I lay eyes upon you
I get a little nervous
Just because I fear
That others near me
Can distinctly hear
The blood rushing to my penis

SINCE OPENING MY EYES
THE AUDIBLE PULSE
OF MY PENIS
CAN BE HEARD BY
THE MASSES
POUNDING TO THE BEAT
OF YOUR NAME

Explode

While I thought that I had been
Walking on the wild side
Maybe I had been tame and reserved?
Just recently you gave me the confidence and pride
Needed to send revealing pics of excitement and seduction
While keeping a romance hidden through obstruction

You are driving me wild
Enough to take these chances
Crazy enough
To take these uncalculated risks

The warmth you have kindled inside of me
Is boiling and truth be told
This anxiety and anticipation you are building
Forces slow movements below my belt, so I don't explode

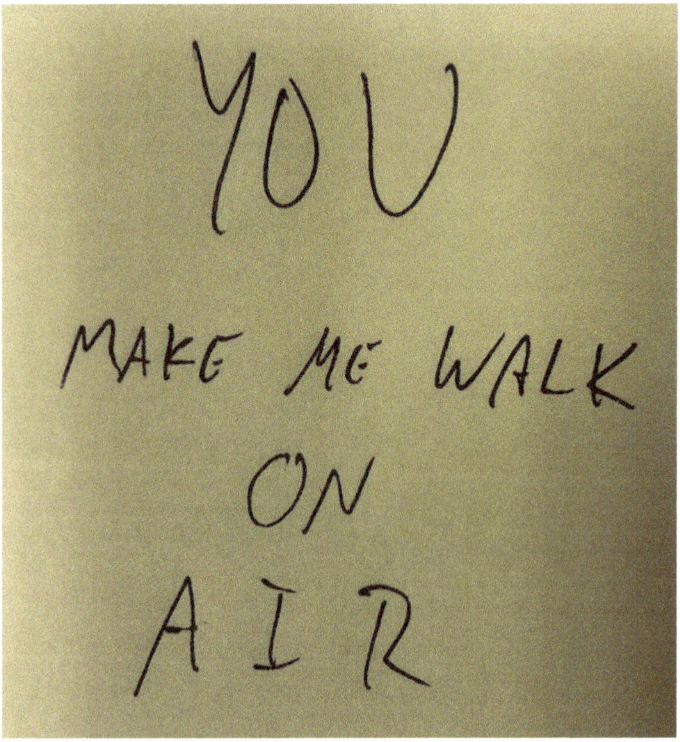
YOU
MAKE ME WALK
ON
AIR

Fascination

Your image significantly increases
The blood flow to my johnson
Like Never Before

Sight of your shape
Pulsates my pelvis
To shake on the floor

Previously feeling this rare
Search was unreasonable
I feel this No More

Just be Aware
That *ALL* my extremities are
Fascinated while Titillated by you

Ever so Completely
Foolishly Breathtaken
Fascinated while Stimulated by you

THE STUNNING SMILE
ON YOUR SILHOUETTE
KEEPS ME RUNNING
TO CONNEXXXTIONS

Fruits

DAMN your Delicious Delights!
My mouth is salivating
My lips are itching
Pants pulsating to the sight
Testicles begging for flight
I wish I may, I wish I might
Taste your moistened fruits tonight

TO CONTEMPLATE
THAT YOU ARE NOT
DIVINE?
UTTER
FOOLISHNESS

YOU
COULD NOT BE
AVERAGE
EVEN
IF YOU WANTED SO

Gaga

I'm so astronomically Gaga
I wish to Transport you away
My mind is swirling in outer space

Aiming to Buy you dinner/
Place you in a hotel room
We (you) can choose the place

But worry not about the funds!
I will simply rob a bank
Wearing a pair of your unwashed panties
In attempt to conceal my face

I WANNA

SUCK UPON YOUR TOES
NIBBLE ON YOUR INSTEP
LICK AND DROOL
ACROSS YOUR FOREFOOT
HOLD AND CARESS YOUR
TENDER HOOF
GLIDE MY LIPS SLOWLY
ALONG YOUR HEEL
POLISH YOUR TOOTSIE UNTIL
THE SHINE REVEALS

"Right"

Gift Of Scarf

This fantasy is actually taking place
Seems like a dream with your pie smashed into my face
I can't believe this happened; how could one throw this away?
Contain and Restrain me, force me to stay
Your movements and your taste have me crying out for more
Can't move my hands or legs, but the playful abuse is what I adore
Choke me, Stroke me—your wonderland strikes me as surreal
Choke me, Stroke me—Tease me and Tickle me until I squeal

Tighten your scarf around my wrists
No worries, I don't plan to leave
Place the sleep mask over my eyes
Sensation is heightened when I cannot see
Tie my ankles to the bedpost with your pants
I don't see the need to stand quickly
Tighten your hold on me
I don't want to go

TASTE BUDS
ARE TITILLATING
TO TOUCH
YOUR
IVORY SKIN

Glide

I want to glide my fingers across the small of your model back
Glide my moistened forefinger down the crack of your bottom.
I prefer to nibble upon the side of your neck
Before I allow my tongue
To follow my forefinger

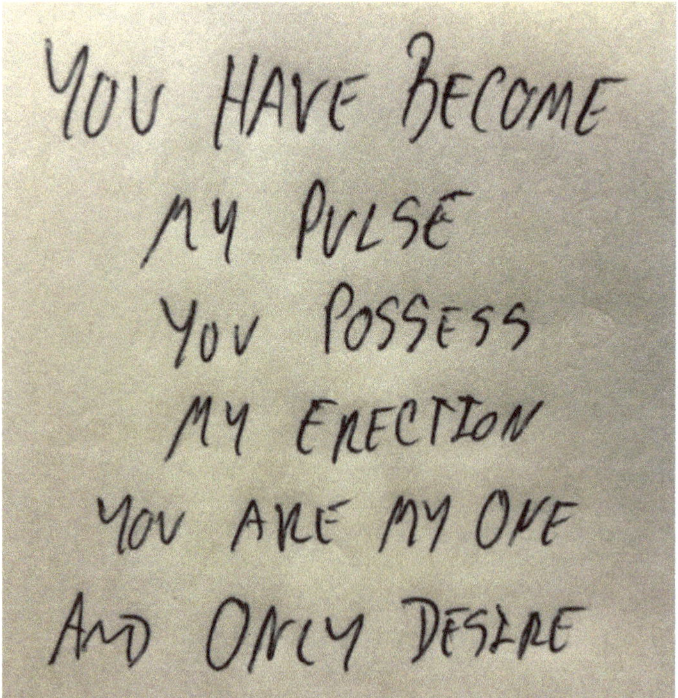
YOU HAVE BECOME
MY PULSE
YOU POSSESS
MY ERECTION
YOU ARE MY ONE
AND ONLY DESIRE

Heartbeat

How blissfully wonderful it feels
To possess and satisfy the desire
To know all your delightful details
To learn every fascinating landscape
Within the wistful world inside of you
For as I would swear, I could not possibly
Crave your touch more than I yearn for that
Right Now
I have a wicked hunch that the pulse profoundly
beating beneath the zipper of my slacks
Will be pulsating at incredible volumes again tomorrow

MY EYES TELL ME
THAT YOUR BODY
IS MAGIC

Hidden Books on The Shelf

I have been admiring her from afar before
Silently holding feelings for her in my soul
But she was a married woman—couldn't even knock on her door
Until her husband Paid for strange pleasure—allowing me to console
Ah, Yes. I recall…
First day at my new school
I was spellbound by the librarian
I remember trying not to drool
As the strides of her walk were utopian
Ah, Now,
Upon our flirting she sent me a "classy" pic
My heart rate increased significantly fast
I replied with my own First dirty pic
My original pleasure will Surely soon be surpassed
We find ourselves exchanging exciting pictures
Sending innumerous images everyday
I can now easily see myself with her
Currently stumbling to find impressive words to say
Every single book she holds has magic
Her body Literature excites my groin
Her almond eyes looking upon me are ecstatic
Our built anticipation we must conjoin
I want to read her hidden Literature
I want to study her body curvature
I want to inhale the sweet scent of her skin
I want to excite her jubilant laughter from within

Hyperventilating

You lift your mask to whisper
Lean in to share a secret
Between you and I
Breathing is heavy
Sounds are low
I've grown so close to you
Surely you see my thinking
Has just become incoherent
As you whirl in my hopes and my desires
I begin to hyperventilate
I feel your breath on my neck
Yet I couldn't hear a word you said
My zipper pokes out while my head still spins
This secret of ours should never have to end

I SEE ECSTASY
THE WAY YOUR LIPS MOVE
I PRAISE AND WORSHIP
THE SOUND OF YOUR WORDS

In Motion

Her majestic presence lightens the world
Her movements displayed while walking are captivating
Similar to falling stars
The elegance magnetizes minds
The population is aware of their beauty
As the fire illuminates the dark sky
Every time I witness her charisma in motion
I make a wish and feel the flames in my pants
She radiates the most innocently erotic feeling I know
I wish to bring it everywhere with me
Study her cashmere skin in the sunlight
Become intoxicated under her righteous aura moonshine
Her gravitational pull centers me
When her astonishment makes me dizzy
As I enjoy the observation of her elegance
And the blissful environment she creates
I am thankful for my amazing fortune
That we have available such visible exquisiteness
While possessing the eyes to witness it

YOUR NON-BLEMISHED
NOSE BEGS ME TO
BITE AND NIBBLE
UPON YOUR EXOTIC
EARLOBE
TO IGNITE AN
INVITING SMILE

In Orbit

My world revolves around you
You are the sun providing light
You can be my moon providing alluring intrigue
Within the darkness encircling me
The most amazing part of your magnetism
Reflects that my eyes weren't even open
When they were drawn toward you
The wrenching pull withdraws
Flowing compliments and reminders of blatant truths
That You are Beautiful
    You are Divine
    You are Exquisite
    You Are Enough! More than Enough.
Now that you have lifted me
I can't get enough of all of you

YOUR WICKEDNESS
HAS SPARKED A FIRE
WITHIN MY LOINS

I SEE YOU SMILE
I TWITCH AND DANCE
TO FAN THE
    FLAMES

In The Skies

Looking for you in the night sky
For every shooting star I see
Your silhouette promises to drop your
Victoria Secret panties an inch
Revealing more skin to tease
Your tempting image is always near me
Amplifying the effect of your seductive powers
Showing your ivory skin, luring "I hope you like?"
Anticipation has me hoping this night gives a meteor shower

YOU ARE THE GRAIL
I WANT TO DRINK YOUR FLUIDS
GARGLE WITH YOUR JUICES
TASTE OUR TIME
AS IT STREAMS DOWN MY CHIN

Insane

Your provocative appearance and appealing personality
Are raising serious questions to ask myself

Have I lost my mind?
Have I misplaced my sanity?
Have I fumbled by rationality?

Because I frequently and willfully
Search and seek to meet you
And then when I find you
You steal my oxygen
Every time I try to breathe

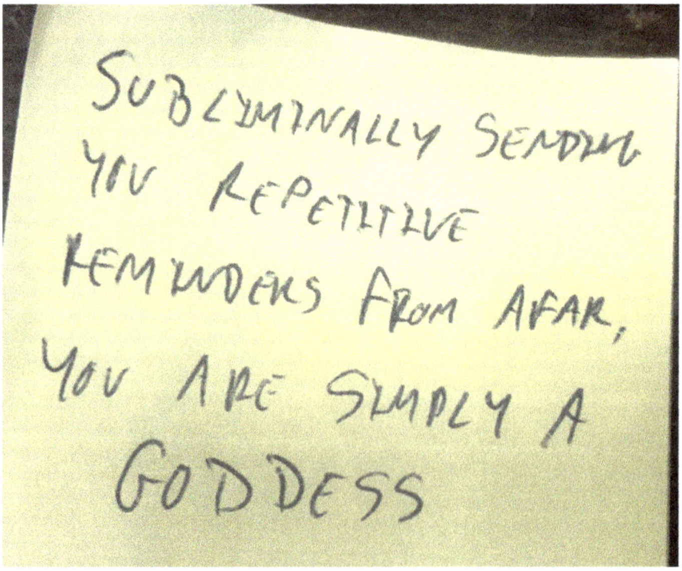
SUBLIMINALLY SENDING
YOU REPETITIVE
REMINDERS FROM AFAR,
YOU ARE SIMPLY A
GODDESS

Just A Glance

While your appetizing physical form and shape
Have not left my mind's eye
Since we first crossed paths at orientation
Several years ago
Your desired essence
Has not left set of sensual cravings
Since you glanced my way

TONGUE IS TICKLING
TO SUPPLY LUBE
ALONG YOUR UNDERBOOB
BEFORE SWIFTLY SHIFTING
TO THE SMALL OF YOUR BACK
GLIDING TASTE BUDS
DOWN YOUR CRACK

Just Asking

Surprisingly not that far from this room
I can faintly hear your melody
I only hope that your music is for me
I know the lyrics to all your songs
Remember each word you say

I have told you previously
I have been admiring you from afar
Held affection for you in silence
Prepping me to embark upon this quest
To become a conqueror

Today
Must put my shyness behind
Take a big step forward this time
Need to set you free from him
Must flip the page to begin our time
Can still keep out of public eye if you like
Will sacrifice what it takes for us to survive
Throwing rocks at windows to turn your mind
Vision tunneled straight forward for a piece of the prize
Bringing you glasses filled with Coffee Wine
I'm dancing on my bed, I'm juggling with our fire
I am on my knees begging for your time
Glance my way; I can open your eyes
Personal Freedom is what you will find
Inform me of your filthy desires
And I am likely to comply
I am sending you the signs
All my limbs have been tied
Waiting for you to make me blind

I'm asking to hold your hand
I'm wanting to rub your feet
Am I moving too fast again?
I'm seeking to massage your thighs
I'm sweating to bite your backside
Maybe I am moving too fast again
But maybe I have known you long enough?

But if you are uncomfortable
I can wait
Excruciatingly
Humiliatingly
I can wait

WITH EVERY BOOK I CLOSE

I CRAVE THE TICKLE OF YOUR

GROOMED PUBIC PAD

UPON MY NOSTRILS

YOUR INNER THIGHS SQUISHING

TOGETHER MY CHEEKS

THERE EXISTS NOT
ENOUGH INK TO CONCEAL
THESE POETIC ADMIRINGS
THAT BARE YOUR NAME

Merely Wishes

We knew that you had to hurry so we redressed quickly
I gazed to admire momentarily as your curves pleased my sight
Still licked my lips to the taste of wine and whiskey
How I wished we could have another glass, and I could hold you tight
I understand. I knew that you were leaving for Arizona
I understand. These to be long days apart will seem to be misery
I understand that you will return, and we will have another dance
I understand and took a shot to what our futures may bring

My only want is to hold you tight
Keep you here within my arms
Your eyes lit by Eucalyptus candlelight
But I have walked you down, and your car is now gone

Even more so now my loins burn for you with fire
Your yells, laughter, and fluids have only fueled my desire
Damn, I wish you could have stayed with me
But I still understand that it had to be
Your hair will now be freshly groomed for you to fly away
Yet even before that trim your exciting appeal made me wish that you
could stay
I understand that this will be a long, excruciating week
But I understand in order to raise your children peacefully this has to be

It may be selfish; I just wish that I could hold you tight
And keep you off that plane
Convince you that we flow so well together that it may be right
I just hope that you feel the same
Man, I just wish that I could hold you tight
You could lay your breasts upon my chest until the night becomes
light

I HAVE SWAM ACROSS
AN OLYMPIC-SIZE POOL
FILLED WITH USED
BOTTLES OF ASTROGLIDE
LEFT EXHAUSTIVELY BARE
— SINCE YOU FIRST
SPOKE MY NAME

More Lube Required

There is an emptiness when you are away
An itch in my palms where your glutes should be
I want you to Dominate me
Humiliate me
Recognize me as your property
I wish for your fingernails to scratch down my back
I vow to make your toes curl
While my lips are between your legs
Inspiring some heavy panting of your breath
Accept my best before rebuilding me to your liking
Construct me as I am yours
My eyes will always be amazed
Witnessing every melodic stride you land
But Rest Assured sweetheart—
It is not only your breathtaking body
It has always been your Blinding, Bright characteristics
I would have fallen This hard with my eyes Wide Shut

As now that I am vividly aware
That such a Powerful stimulant as yourself exists
How could I Not become addicted?
Dreaming of you has become dangerous
Through excessive requirements of potions and lotions
In which I indulge climactically often

My World

Every time I step on these blue grounds
She has become a pleasant distraction
I lose my mind to admire and fantasize her all throughout the day.
She consumes my thoughts
She dominates my dreams
She has become my World
Oh, I pray her world hopes to believe

POLAROIDS OF YOUR
PLEASANTRIES HAVE POWDERED
PIXIE DUST ACROSS MY
EYELIDS.
CAN'T ALLOW MYSELF
TO BLINK

Not The Same

You need not be afraid
To leave your past behind
You have open arms waiting for you
You have unzipped pants begging for you

You are both a fierce, uncontrollable fire
And a surreal, perpetual sunlight
Without question
The rarest woman in my world

You have imprinted on me
Leaving marks and pieces on my skin
Giving images radiating light in my steps
You have altered my outlook
Seems like things will not be the same
It appears that I will not be the same

BEEN RUBBING MYSELF RAW
SINCE YOU OPENED MY EYES
YOU HAVE ME DRAWING COUNTLESS
BOTTLES OF ASTROGLIDE
GLIDING TO YOU FRESH
SLIDING TO YOU SMOOTH
OOHHH NNOOOO!!
BELIEVE I'M GONNA SPEW!

Damn It

Generating blood flow
You're rushing blood to my knob
Generating blood flow
Zipper protrusion going up
Another pic excites my prick
With each sent photo, my zipper lifts

Still frames keep building anticipation
Schlong tingling for consummation
Eagerly awaited celebration
Could we exchange nude still frames at night?
Wish to glide lips over your skin tonight
Mouth salivating to lick you right

Scrape my cheeks along your thighs
Glancing up to look into your eyes
Moaning out and twisting up sideways
Noting the spot where your moisture stays
Hand up cupped upon your breast
Right hand supporting your tush to rest
Nothing but your juices around my lips
Your glow of satisfaction will be lit
Give you time to come down from your high
Fine features burning from the inside

Your pics leave my loins burning now
Wish our pants were coming down
Staring at your ivory skin
I can be found gawking again
At your surreal boobs and bottom
Balls are bubbling can't stop 'em

Gathering your pictures
I'm gonna blow my load
Gathering your pictures
Damn it—Going to Explode!

GAWKING TO GLIDE
MY LIPS —
ALONG YOUR HIPS
PRIOR TO FEASTING
UPON THE PRIZE

IF YOU COULD ONLY SEE
THE STRENGTH OF MY GAZE
UPON YOU WHEN
YOUR ALMOND EYES ARE
FOCUSED ELSEWHERE
YOU COULD IDENTIFY THE
SOUND OF FLUIDS
FLUSHING TO MY PHALLUS

On Guard

You have set my sword ablaze
I cannot control the flames
I doubt my weaponry has ever fired so forcefully
Until I saw your glance and began packing heat
Yet,
Simultaneously,
Your flames can also be calming
Tranquilizing the troubling devilry
Your movements construct

YOUR KILLER CHARISMA
AND PLEASING PERSONA
ARE FETCHING

Plan To Hold

I want you to know that I plan to hold you
Carry you as far as my legs will carry us
I seek to cure everything that hinders you
Care for everything that aches you
Continue to repetitively remind you that

You are Indeed Astonishing
Open your almond eyes to see
That you are nuts to doubt your beauty
I will be forced to repeat myself until
You see and believe in yourself

Breathe in—as you have stolen my wind

Allow yourself to move on to the next chapter
Turn your book to the next page
Find a story that you find interesting
Find a story that may be worth your time

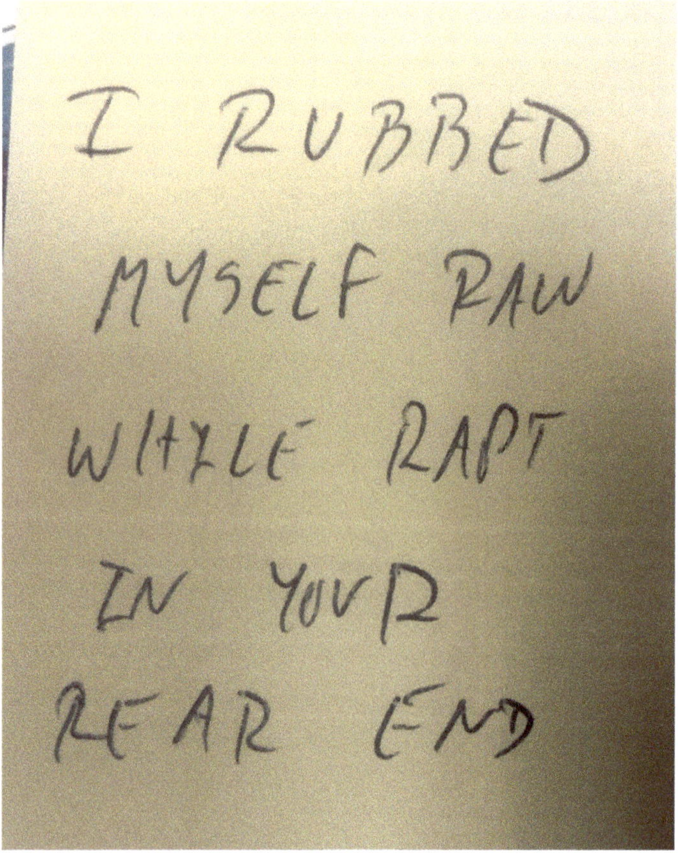
I RUBBED
MYSELF RAW
WHILE RAPT
IN YOUR
REAR END

Poor Johnny

I Can't Figure Out How to walk into the school library
Without lustfully staring and gawking at you
I Can't Figure Out How to catch a whiff of your perfume scent
Without my mouth salivating heavily
I Can't Figure Out How to glance upon your blouse
Without staring at and studying your chest
Before sending a rush of blood toward my zipper
I Can't Figure Out How to glance my eyes across your pants
Without dreaming that you were wearing less
Consequently causing my zipper to rise quicker
I Can't Figure Out How to conserve some of this Astroglide
Without making Johnny red to the point of rawness

SOLIDLY SURE
THAT I AM THE REASON
YOU ARE STRIP TEASIN'
— SHOOTS BLOOD TO
    MY SHAFT

Reading Fluency

I seek to read All the Literature
Held within your library
Open the gate for me
You know that I am primed for this adventure
To dine upon your delicacy
Open your legs for me
No hair upon my lip
No hair upon your mound
No inhibitions to prevent
Groaning and moaning sounds
Keeping your mind flying free
While our clothes lay flat as ground

THE MAGIC
IN YOUR MARVELOUS
MOVEMENTS
KEEPS THE FLAP MATERIAL
OF MY BOXER BRIEFS
IN PERPETUAL MOTION

Relax

There is only you and I
Take my hand
Follow me into your office
I wrap my arms around you for a warm embrace
My chest is burning
You could melt inside my arms
To raise the heat even farther
I place my hands Firmly below your belt loops
Allowing me to forcefully cup each of your perky glutes
"OH SHIT! THERE'S A WINDOW!"

I don't believe anyone saw
Most of the remarkable, precious moments
Such as these often pass unnoticed
I could have stood there just channeled in
To your laughter and smile for hours
Even if we had nothing to say
I felt comfortable smiling with you

SHE RESIDES IN MY MIND
SEDUCTIVELY DANCING
IN MY THOUGHTS.

SOMETIMES SHE WILL PAUSE,
AND SHE CATCHES ME
STARING ADMIRABLY.
AS I STUMBLE TO
SEIZE THE MOMENT,
SHE GIGGLES BEFORE TEASING
WITH HER CELESTIAL LAMBADA

Religion

She is divine
And I am the bishop
Amidst her army of worshippers

I lead the orchestra in hymns honoring her stride
I take the mic to recite praises in her name
The flow in her formal attire commands attention
The softness of her dark hair deserves affection
The elegance and grace of her appearance in public
Originates awe, causing the seas to split

I adore the ground upon which she walks
I idolize the seats upon which she places her tush
I worship the mattress on which she chooses to lie
Sleekly and discreetly, she has become my religion

I KNEEL BEHIND YOU
WITH HANDS CLAPPED, RAISED,
   PALMS PERSPIRING,
PRAISING, RAVING FORWARD...
BEFORE SILENCE - THE DIVINE
MY FINGERTIPS STREAM DOWN
THE SMALL OF YOUR BACK —
   SLIDE-TO-GLIDE WITHIN TO
   PART YOUR CRACK —
PREPARE TO WORSHIP

Royal Court

It is possible to unintentionally make the world difficult.
People can be the worst, while starting over can be utter terrifying.

However,
I think that you will drain yourself beyond recognition if you choose
to remain in a toxic relationship.
You will be made to believe that you do Not deserve better—
that you do Not deserve to be treated Respectfully, with admiration
and
praise. You should be treated accordingly, like a Queen.
Madam,
I cordially invite you to become Royalty within my Kingdom.

Salivating

Your eyes demand the attention that I give you
My sights provide you with the praise that you deserve
When my stare is enamored by you
There could be utter chaos and destruction
Taking place all around me
Yet I wouldn't close my eyes for a blink

I know that you have been treated wrongly
I know that you were devastated as a result
But I can't remember softly conversing
With a such a strong, stellar woman
Despite experiencing such a hardening, troublesome past
I have unprecedentedly opened myself to you
Thus, I seek to savor every piece of your art to satisfaction

THE FLIGHT OF
YOUR FRECKLES
FANCIES MY PHALLUS

Salvation

You have become my necessity
You have become my desire
You have become my world
Your name has become my most esteemed word
In any of the sentences I compose
Devoted to repetition of placing your name
And my writing continuously runs me out of ink
You have inspired my writing
Aspiring painter of art?
Sculptor of statues?
Molder of moldings?
I want to hold you as my art
You are my Salvation

SHE HOLDS

MAGIC IN HER EYES
CHARM UPON HER CHEST
WITH A BEWITCHING
BACKSIDE
THAT KEEPS MY
JOHNSON JUMPING!

She

She is a mesmerizing enigma
Consisting of what we can only guess are
Stars, astounding features, intoxicating laughter,
Sugar, creamer, and exquisite literature.

THE TREASURE
IN YOUR ALMOND EYES
URGES ME TO SEARCH

SKILLFULLY IN YOUR
EVERY CREASE AND CREVICE
FOR PRICELESS
KNOWLEDGE

Showers

I am thinking about you right now
After I dreamed about you while in the shower
I am constantly thinking about you

Thoughts that warm my skin
Dreams that tingle my insides
Hopes to hold you outdoors under the stars
Wants to see your dark eyes lit by the moon

Ponderings that remind me of how magnificent your curves are
How impeccable your stature appears
How sultry the sleekness of your skin ignites
How admirable your care and compassion comes off
How addictive your smile and laughter intoxicates
These fairy tales wake with me in the morning
Dance in my dreams at night
Walk beside me every tick of the clock in between
My essence sends you: Sincere warmth
True care
Definitive desire
I am here.
Fantasizing of you
Before, during, and after the shower

PROMISES AND
SELF PRAISES OF YOUR
FELLATIO SKILLS
KEEP BOTH OF MY
HEADS BOBBING

Sinners We Are

I tend to wake up in the midst of sleeping
And I have begun to feel this ache for you that is deepening
My lower gut is Pumping and Jumping, or so it seems to be
As my thoughts are thumping with images of your extremities
I have had to take care of my own business before I can close my eyes
again
I only wonder if you think of me following the choice to make your-
self moist and moan in sin

Somewhere

You belong amongst a mass of red roses
Your enchanting, robust lipstick will be an alluring compliment to
the ensemble
Your shade of maroon belongs

Somewhere near me
Somewhere within my vicinity
Somewhere away from worry and anxiety
Somewhere away from arguments and toxicity
Somewhere to spread your wings and fly free
Somewhere where you are meant to be
Somewhere near me

I FEEL THE NEED
TO NIBBLE ON YOUR NIPS
CLAMP 'EM DOWN!
RESTRAIN MY LIMBS

Spent

Just lie here
Spent
Share Time with me
Share skin with me
Let me remind you
Of All the things
I Adore about you

Steadfast

You placed yourself above me
With your legs pressed against my ears
Your cries of excitement and approvals
My neighbors were likely to hear

The movements and gestures of our dance
Sent my legs flying to deliver like mythical reindeer
I had dreamed and prepared myself faithfully
For this magical rendezvous for many years

Inhaling and Exhaling so in this
Simply blissful fantasy
Has caused my zipper to swing dance
Focused steadfast while reaching out toward your rear

THOUGHTS OF YOUR
TALENTED LIPS
ARE SENDING
THUNDEROUS
PUMPS OF BLOOD
TO MY PENIS

Stunning

You are Certainly above the common woman
Therefore, common gestures of affection simply will not suffice
You can Free yourself of your troublesome current companionship
Perhaps you have embarked upon sincere understanding and compassion
I blatantly admire your essence and stature
Standing statuesque as Powerfully and Majestically Stunning as you have become

LEANING AND REACHING
FORWARD, YOUR SMALL SHIRT
   COULD NOT CONCEAL
DIVINE SKIN UPON THE
   SMALL OF YOUR BACK
SENSUAL SIGHT BECKONED
MY TASTE BUDS AND NASAL OPENINGS
TO PROVIDE MOISTURE AND WARMTH
   ALL ALONG YOUR CRACK

Surely

Surely, sugarbutt,
You understand that you are golden
Your Delicious curves are not deserved by most men

But I understand that after decades
You may have become immune to the mistreatment
You've gotten so used to your broken shadow
So accustomed to finding your flying feet in cement
That you could not swiftly or even hesitantly run away
Remained too just scared to pursue happiness
I inhale deeply, trying to prove deserving of the grail
'Tis a challenge to impress without soaking of sappiness

I WANNA
SUCK UPON YOUR TOES
NIBBLE ON YOUR INSTEP
LICK AND DROOL
ACROSS YOUR FOREFOOT
HOLD AND CARESS YOUR
TENDER HOOF
GLIDE MY LIPS SLOWLY
ALONG YOUR HEEL
POLISH YOUR TOOTSIE UNTIL
THE SHINE REVEALS

"Left"

Tell Me, Have You Seen Her?

Hey, have you seen her?
Have you heard what she is wearing today?
Floating along her path
In a stunning casual blouse I'd say

Dancing through her strides in heavy denim
Length to reveal her ankles—my pulse begins to change
No socks, No tan lines, No bunions
No fungal infection tarnishing her name

Glorious 'tis the Footwear season!
Goodbye boots, to warm sandal wear at its peak
She is walking toward me—my jaw is now dropping
I want to gaze into her boobs, but my eyes can't leave her feet

Strap-back sandals with traceable veins
Obtained via jogging habitually
Her foot width and arch hold an impressive sight to see
Influences my self-pleasure/gratification significantly

Tenderness

I want to see the woman
With the scars on her superb chest
With the marks within her head from overthinking
Aching not completely entirely from heavy, habitual drinking

I want to heal the cracks and tears in her heart
From spending years with the wrong person
I want to care for the pain held within her body
Concealed through her kindness, compassion, and loyalty

I will do everything within my human power
To supply her with tenderness
And just be with her

SINCE YOU'VE SENT
SIGHTS OF YOUR SEDUCTIVE,
SIN-WISHING SKIN
I AM FORCED TO FIGURE
MASS QUANTITIES OF
ASTROGLIDE
INTO MY BUDGET

Testimonial

In this moment
Pulsating and Throbbing Firm
I yearn to be inside your
Delightful, warm, moist, delicious
Fire upon the pedestal between your
Athletically-toned thighs
Damn it appears to be time
To embark on yet another excursion
Testimonially enhanced by Astroglide

The Library

Early morning—coffee steaming
Discreetly placing your cup upon your desk
I had that same strange dream last night
I wore your name in ink upon my chest

Told me you had a boob job
Damn, it is warm in here
Would you like to meet somewhere?
Is it warm in here?
Are you warm down there?
Anticipation…

Maroon lips and coffee wine
Grey Goose Vodka in your hair
Michelob Ultra under the sun
Sipping on Screwdrivers until school year's end

Stand beside me—take my hand
Blue skies are seen overhead
I step inside to see you, my muse
All the signs are pointing me there

All your movements have indeed seduced me
All I can do is reply
Someone took you for granted
But you know that I won't
You Know that I will not
We need this

I can meet you in the library
The nonfiction aisle is bare

Loveable Loretta behind your desk
I can see you there

Cherry lips with sweet white wine
Seagram's Seven and seven in your hair
Sipping on Salty Dogs under the sun
Yearning for the school year's end

Candy lips with bourbon over ice
Moonshine in your hair
Crown and Coke under the sun
Itching for the school year's end

TINKERINGS OF

YOUR TITS
TICKLE UPON
MY TESTICLES

AS YOU HAVE
IGNITED THIS BURNING
WITHIN MY LOINS
I AWAIT THE HEAT
FOUND ON MY SHOULDERS
AS YOU DRIP HOT WAX

UPON MY TRAPS

Time

For the first time since I've known you
Your hand is not held by someone else
His foolish mistake opens the opportunity
For me to offer consolation by holding you close to me
I feel the need to put us on the table
For the first time we are both available
My arms are open as my zipper is poking away
Patiently throbbing to detonate

Previous crashes brought our fires together
Playful enthusiasm keeps flames through any weather
Ground is dry to join me on my picnic blanket
Just tell me what you want, and I will make it
Do you prefer sweet or spicy?
Favor innocent or nasty?
I want to give you what you want
But I need to bake with what you flaunt
What could all these enticing actions be foreboding?
Unprecedented blood flow to my groin before exploding?

It is just a matter of time—Before things go Boom
It is just a matter of time—Until we have our own room
And that time, my dear, Certainly cannot get here too soon

Will this be our time? Can this be our time?
If it is not, it is fine
But can this be our Time?

I PRESENT TO YOU
A DOZEN RED ROSES
TO GROW BENEATH THE SOIL
AS YOU HAVE CREATED
A RUSH OF RED BLOOD
TO GROW BENEATH MY
ZIPPER _ A
PROTRUSION WILL SHOW
_THAT BEATS TO THE
RHYTHM OF YOUR
NAME

Tingle

My cheeks began to Tingle
When I first saw you
Years ago
Oh, how they couldn't wait
To be pressed between your inner thighs

Too Frequently

Your intoxicating smile soothes me like Cabernet
Just a glance and my guard and inhibitions drop to the floor
The fact that you exist in my world inspires me to dream
The fact that I have been moved by sound of your voice influences
My decision to frequently purchase and utilize Astroglide

I SWAY GENTLY DOWN
YOUR FICTION AISLE
WITH A VIOLIN
UNDER MY CHIN
PLAYING WITH A GRIN
PULLING SOFTLY FOR

YOUR SMILE

Uncommon Smile

It is hard to tell if you are happy
Or possibly hiding feelings of sadness
Tempting definition of your soft lips
Inviting between where your pearly whites sit
Perhaps I have told you a line to make you laugh
Maybe you are waiting for a moment of awkwardness to pass
Regardless, I just can't seem to get enough of it
Your addictively intoxicating smile—one can only love it

INHALE.
EXHALE.
REALIZE YOUR
EXQUISITE
VALUE

Undeniably Enough

My World revolves around you
You are the Sun providing light
You can be the moon at times
Providing glowing eroticism
Amidst the dark encircling me

The most amazing part of your magnetism
Is that my eyes weren't even open
When they were drawn to your glow
The pull toward your power withdraws
Frequent reminders of flattering words
And flatly Blatant truths:

That You Are Beautiful
  You Are Divine
  You Are Exquisite
  You Are Enough
  MORE Than Enough!
Your smile and laughter have lifted me to see
That I Cannot seem to get Enough of You

WHEN I WAS DAZZLED
BY SIGHT OF YOUR SKIN
SENT ON THE FIRST PHOTO
YOU SPED DIRECTION OF
BLOOD FLOW TO MY EXTREMITIES
YOUR OPEN EYES
CHANGED EVERYTHING

Unforgettable Beauty

From truth to fiction
From beauty to elegance
From astonishing to exquisite
From loyalty to stunning
From moving to grasping
Her Literature holds it all
Her characters tell my favorite story
Every word draws me and my extremities close
Each detail held me captive
Her features
Her attributes
Pulled me into her tale
It is a timeless story I can read repetitively

Unpossible

Allow your sultry curves
To stay in their seductive state
Do Not let any harmful words
Or devastating actions
From certain harmful morons
Or devastating dickheads
Affect your astounding appeal.
The rare, alluring attraction of your
Appetizingly astonishing assets
Leaves little, if any, possibility
Of leading one astray
Thoughts of doubt do Not
Belong in your brain

IMAGES OF YOUR
MAGNIFICENT MOUNDS
MARVELOUSLY MOVE
MY MISSLE
MONUMENTOUSLY

Vitality

I can't seem to get enough of you
I think that I may need you
You constantly fulfill my desires
You constantly provide me with what I need.

Your essence and aura awaken feelings
Within me that I never once thought
Were a vital necessity

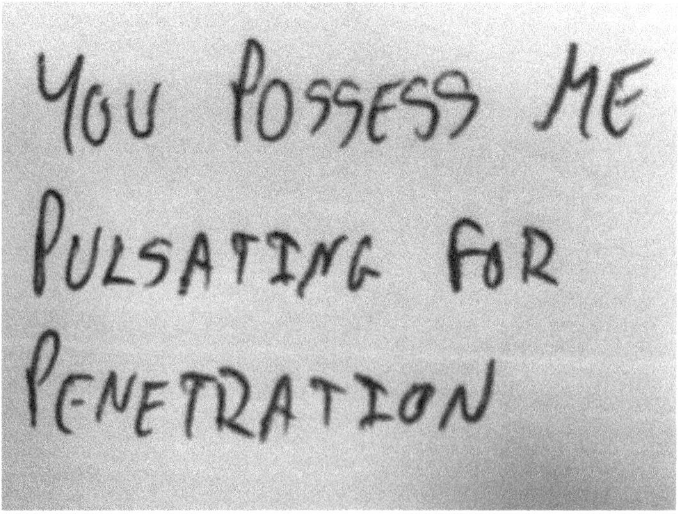
YOU POSSESS ME
PULSATING FOR
PENETRATION

Volcano

Despite your seductive silhouette
Living beside me
Every time my eyes land on you in person
I feel something tingling inside me
Something warming in my groin
Something burning in my loins
Like glowing lava churning inside
Of a rumbling volcano waiting to erupt

Your magic has me falling
Falling faster than I ever imagined possible
Falling so deeply into your fire
But Before becoming engulfed in flames
I prefer to run barefoot on coals for miles
To prove the validity of my raging desire

IT STRIKES ME
SO SEDUCTIVELY
HOW RAPIDLY YOUR EYES
HAVE ORCHESTRATED
MY EVERY
CARNAL DESIRE

Voluptuous Lick

My plans are to lick you properly
I fantasize of your back off the mattress
As you find it necessary to moan and bite your lip
Your thighs simultaneously vibrate and quiver
I dream of Feasting upon your vag
Anxious to begin applying your moisture upon my lips
Turn your flood into waterfall upon my chin
While drenching the sheets I sleep upon

Walk

I have repeatedly reminded you that you are astonishing
I subliminally screamed for you to "OPEN YOUR EYES!"
As my mouth would open to gaze my eyes upon your chest
Surely, the protruding bulge in the crotch of my pants helped you realize
You possess everything that EVERY man could desire
I held you close in attempts to make you see
The depths of my desire for you are deep indeed
Take my hand and share your eyes
Relax
Breathe
Take a walk with me

What Matters

You make me feel so warm and confident inside
As if nothing we have done before this is important
Everything from our pasts is meaningless
Everything that has come
Everything that has gone
All our failures
All our baggage
We can deal with and accept the results
Only where we find ourselves
NOW
The smiles that we place on the face of one another
The laughs and the giggles that we uprise from the belly of one another
And hopefully the rare snort I can hatch from your nostrils
That is all that matters
I can't wait to walk to you
So we can say goodbye to everyone else to close the day

WHILE IN ARIZONA

UNFORTUNATELY
ARIZONA
I CANNOT REJOICE
FROM SEVERAL STATES AWAY
I HAVE NO CHOICE
FROM SEVERAL STATES AWAY
I HAVE NO VOICE

Air

The smell of her hair
The taste of her mouth
Enjoyment of juice
Feelings of her skin

Seem to have all gotten inside of me
Or into the essential air 'round me
Loretta has become a physical necessity

Amazing

Loretta, *YOU* are Simply Amazing
Sparsely Dusting your Hot Carnal Magic
Sights, Sounds, Smells of High Sensual Instinct
Oh, How Addictive your Taste and Mad Skills!

Blood Rush

Loretta resembled a fine whiskey
I felt esteemed and honored to taste.
One glorious sip of her warmth left
A distinct burn within my chest
And significantly increased the blood flow to my groin

YOU'VE BEEN
MISTREATED
AND
DISTRAUGHT
FOR YEARS-BUT
YOUR SMILE
IS SO DAMN
ADDICTIVE

Brilliance

You need to be with someone
Who brings out the Best
And the sheer Brilliance in you
Not the stress
And the Doubtfulness
He has caused you

Captivating Loretta,
Somehow you don't even realize
That sane people
Look at your impressive stature
And see Nothing but
Brilliance and Eroticism

Clearly

Clearly,
Being with the wrong man
Will force you to doubt your potential.
Obviously,
Being with the wrong man
Will force you to question the effort
And devotion that YOU deserve
In your relationship.
Minds are Spinning

MY FACE NEVER WANTS
TO STRAY FROM THE SIGHT
IN BETWEEN YOUR THIGHS
MY NOSTRILS WILL NEVER
BE TOO MAD
TO STRAY FROM THE TINGLING
TICKLE OF YOUR PAD

Desire

PARANOIA! PARANOIA! PARANOIA!
Cabernet! Caberney! Caber*NAY*!
These bottles of Yellow Tail Red Vino
Go down smoothly, I must say.

Your self-respect and confidence
Must be stronger than any wish
To hold on to hopes of the past
You have definitely glowed differently
You have shined more profusely
You have smiled even more intoxicatingly
You radiate *PASSION* when you are treated properly
While being openly desired carnivorously

I realize that I am imagining the worst
Visualizing my darkest fears while you are away
Do I do this because it is something I deserve?
Twists in the crucifying plot of anguish
Is this paranoia and discomfort some sort of karma?

It is antagonizing to wait calmly and patiently
For something you fear may never happen
But yet are these actions possibly unnecessary?
Whenever this fantasy just seems to be
Everything I could ever desire

I CAN'T LET IT GO

WHILE YOU ARE UNABLE
TO SEE YOUR WINGS
THE WORLD CAN
SEE JUST HOW
BEAUTIFULLY RADIANT
YOU ARE
LORETTA

Dreaming

There are dreams worth
Following and dreams worth
Chasing...

And dreams worth Fighting for
There are also dreams
Of Loretta...

Dreams worth Fighting for,
Even those that tell you to Believe!
Still Some Urge...

Despite not having wings
Becoming determined to grow a pair
And Learning to Fly.

Everyone Knows

Your curves are simply hypnotic
The intriguing way that you move
The enticing way that you consume me

The way that you breathe
It keeps me aroused
You are empowered
I am impassioned
By your every move
Grab my hand under the sun
There is no reason to hide
I'll carry you to the bed from the whiskey bottle
Hold you in my arms, Loretta, each and every night

Don't ask how long I'll be by your side
Don't worry if things between us change
Everything to one another we do confide
Everything that I want bears your name

You keep my head spinning a million miles an hour
Romantic risks you can have me taking
I am found so comfortable around you
Rest your head upon my shoulder
I just want to passionately hold you
We will swing and how we will sway
Until our timeless soundtrack ends

Fade Away

I don't know how else to write this

It's taken a bottle of Cabernet to do this
My eyes are heavy, and my vision is not straight
Attitude too pessimistic
Trying to stay optimistic
I'm not shedding tears, but I am very afraid

Can only give you hopes and promises
While lusting for your curves and firm assets
Maybe it's time that I should drop my pride
Falling so fast is not really my style
I'm holding on to hope, and I don't know why

My tongue is willing to encircle your anus
When your breasts are pressed to my chest
Nothing but the salt in sweat as friction between us
Maybe my wishes need to just fade away
I want to commit to your strong loyalty
Without an opportunity
I'd want to hide in obscurity
I must force my intentions to calmed subtlety

Where am I supposed to go now? What am I supposed to do?
I don't want to pressure, I only want to impress you
Tell me I'm the man that you want to see
Tell me that I could have it all
I just know that I want you, Loretta, and I have to try

Fresh-Ground Caffeine

With the scent of coffee each morning I have grown to think of her,
It seems as if with each sip I begin to daydream.

I can only ponder:
Should I pursue?
Or should I withdraw?
I uneasily wonder:
Should I step back?
Or should I lunge forward?

Like a fugitive, her silhouette glides by, teasing me with her scent and
wonderous delights.
I admirably spectate as she pulls up her loosened shirt and jeans without wearing a belt.

Integrity

You are mesmerizing, Loretta
But your adoring looks
Never stood a chance for air
When compared to
The breathtaking depths
Of your Integrity

YOU ARE THE
HAPPINESS
YOUR FIGURE
THE ECSTASY THAT
I WILL NEVER
LET GO

Jackpot

Loretta,
You deserve someone
Who tries every day
To be deserving
Of the jackpot that is
Happily erotic
And
Vibrantly Resounding—
You.

Just Understand

Just understand
Following your return
Whenever I am able to
Wrap my arms around you
You will hear me regurgitate
That "I missed you"

Just understand
That it translates to state
I have sorely missed you
More than I had imagined
That I ever could possibly
Miss the presence of another

OUR EYES OPENED
AND CHANNELLED
AS WE BOTH
HID HURT
BEHIND OUR SMILES

Lie On Me

Want you to see clearly
Words like *paranoia*
Disrupt my utopia
Visions of you and me
Our skills were built to meet
Oh, can't you understand?
My little sugarpants

Body astonishing
Skills so profound to me
My feelings have grown intense
In challenging circumstance
Promises remain
Will Not bring you pain
Doing everything to say
I won't let you walk away

This Here is all I ever wanted
This Here is all I ever needed
You Here in my arms
Spoken words are preferably
Just unnecessary
They seem to only cause harm

Literature

All my fantasies are erotic
But none as stimulating as you
Never before have I been so inspired
To compose literature and personal-pleasure fantasies
Your essence has become the reason I read and write
Your steamy silhouette pleasantly
Encourages my literacy

FROM THE GRAND CANYON STATE
MY HANDS ARE BOUND
AS I CANNOT TOUCH YOU
MY EARS ARE TAUT AND MUFFED
AS I CANNOT HEAR YOU
MY MOUTH IS STUFFED AND GAGGED
 AS I CANNOT SPEAK
THIS DISCOMFORT WOULD BE TOLERABLE
IF AS MY DOMINATRIX
 YOU COMMAND SADISM
AND ENFORCE MASOCHISM

Locked And Chained

It begins at daybreak
When I open my eyes
I leap toward my cell phone
I lunge to my Apple device
I hope to see a message of your words
I wish to scc a picturc of your skin
It appears as if
You have me Hooked, Bound, and Hanging,
Locked, and Chained from
The cliffs of the Grand Canyon

Moved

I only wish
That you were mine,
But even still
You move me
In such a way
That I lose
ALL control

Never

Never cheat yourself, sweetheart
Never allow Anyone to treat you
Like anything
Below Royalty

No Honey Whiskey

Drinking Cabernet so excessively
Kept me questioning insecurities
Can't call, can't text, no communication
Spinning rancid mind with these restrictions

I view man creating new memories
Tempting to erase infidelities
States away sit utterly helpless
Warmly holding on to physical bliss
Chemistry and addicted to her kiss

She claims it's hot
Temperatures over one hundred
Plans to get some sun and make skin red
Horseback riding away from streets
Memories I cannot compete

But moving of extremities
Matched the move of my dangling keys
Tasty curves so immaculate
Sights and sounds so exquisite
Certain to me whom to be with

Old me and lovely Loretta
We do need to be together
We sure can complete the lap
Riding fresh on bare horseback

THE FOOLISH BELIEF
THAT YOU ARE NOT
GOOD ENOUGH
WILL KEEP YOU IN THE
ARMS OF SOMEONE
NOT WORTHY OF YOUR
PRECIOUS TIME

Some People

Some people
Will praise you
Differently than which
You are accustomed
You will Not be forced
To second-guess
Or question their
Sincerity and honesty
It will simply be known
Trust it
Feelings will indeed
Be That Real
Emotions will flow
That Deeply

Something

Something needs to be said
Something must be said
I kept repeating myself to Shiraz
Excruciatingly
Following her wishes
Adhering to her orders
I can't call her
I can't contact her
While she is away with her children

Out of Fear that she is reuniting and reconciling with him
Out of paranoia that she is enjoying his prowess
Utterly Petrified that this trip is moving them closer together
I feel helpless
I feel alone
As if the walls of my apartment
Were moving in upon me
As if these walls were also moving closer together

Her absence hurts
Her void left terrorizes
This vacation with him and her children
Teases me as if I were a toddler
Waiting to suck on promised candy
Salivating to taste and devour delicious pie
But received next to nothing

The trip mocks me as if they were having a laugh at my expense
The world behind her ridicules me

For Believing that she really wanted to share a dance
For Believing that I actually had a fighting chance

I have to talk this over more with Shiraz
Something needs to be said

YOU SHOULD HAVE
LEFT A LONG TIME AGO
SWEETHEART
BEFORE YOU BEGAN
TO DOUBT YOUR
SELF-WORTH

Tickle

I could never imagine
That anyone could so
Easily make me smile,
Laugh, and
Tickle my dreams
As quickly as you have, Loretta.

Timeless

When I first saw you
landing strides
through your doors,
I finally caught an idea
of what a Timeless Erection
may find essential.

I KNOW YOU'D LIKE TO KEEP
YOUR SADNESS AND GRIEF INSIDE
FOOLING THE WORLD AROUND YOU
    THROUGH YOUR LAUGHTER
    AND INTOXICATING SMILE
YOU CAN BE HONEST WITH ME
    I WON'T JUDGE YOU
    I WON'T HARM YOU
    I WON'T DOUBT YOU
    I UNDERSTAND YOU
    I WON'T DISCREDIT YOU
    DESPITE IT ALL
        I CARE

Truth

After everything
a woman of your
extraordinary beauty
and enchanting essence
has been through—
You deserve a Stellar man
who means what he says.

Sincerely,
Truth

NO NEED TO FALL
BACK INTO
BETRAYING ARMS
EXCLUSIVELY DUE
TO FAMILIARITY

Waiting

I will wait for
You because
Honestly, I don't
Want anyone
Else.

I sit and wait for
You because
Sincerely You are
Superior to the
Rest.

Whatever

I fell too quickly to prepare for this
Went from communicating frequently to Ceasing to Exist
Sights and samples of your delicious goods have proven to be dangerous
Causing Craziness—I'm hoping my mind can handle this

Communication is so vital in order to survive
When taken away, pictures of the worst appear in Mind's eye
Positively wishing to find my face squished between your thighs
Still chasing my dream, I can't see myself saying goodbye

I'll do whatever it takes—
The hair that was donned above my lips has since been shaved
I'll do whatever it takes—
So my lips can glide smoothly across your pad when we misbehave
I'll do whatever it takes—
To place that contagious smile back upon your face
I'll do whatever it takes—
To make your voice and laughter heard loud around this place
I'll do whatever it takes—
Reassure you there is somewhere to go if you want to escape
I'll do whatever it takes—
For you to hear these words that I can't say across these states
Tell me what it will take, Loretta

THE MOON ENVIES YOU
BUT SO DOES THE SUN
YOU ARE SO RARE
SO MESMERIZING

Wonderwall

Even after swimming and gargling in this Cabernet,
Aside from drowning and possible nausea,
I am Frightened and Scared;
Because you have grown to mean more to me
Than any other person—much more than I intended.
You are now everything I think about,
Everything I want,
Everything I desire.
Despite singing the mainstream song aloud,
Just recently becoming familiar with the definition,
You have certainly become my Wonderwall.

YOUR PICTURED,
DEFINED CALVES
DESERVE CARESSING CARE
CRITICAL OBSERVATION
AND CLOSE STUDY

Worshipped

Loretta is Not
to be placed
in any corners
or exist merely
as an afterthought.
Not to be seen
as a "failsafe"
or a "backup plan"
We must Open our Eyes!
She is the gift—
she is the present.
She is a goddess
deserving to be Worshipped.

ALMOST AS IF
YOU KNEW -

MY MOST MAGNIFICENT

WEAKNESS WAS

TEMPTATION

You Knew

When I saw you
I fell for you, and
You smiled
Because
You knew

TELL ME THAT YOU HAVE

NOT BEEN FIGHTING
SO HARD FOR
HIS DIVIDED ATTENTION
— THAT YOU HAVE FORGOTTEN
YOUR VALUE

POSTCLIMACTIC

After

WHY?
Keep granting the man NONdeservant with Chance,
After Chance,
After Chance,
After Chance,
After Fucking Chance,
After you have been shown Numerous Times before that he Does
Not Value,
Does Not Deserve YOU!

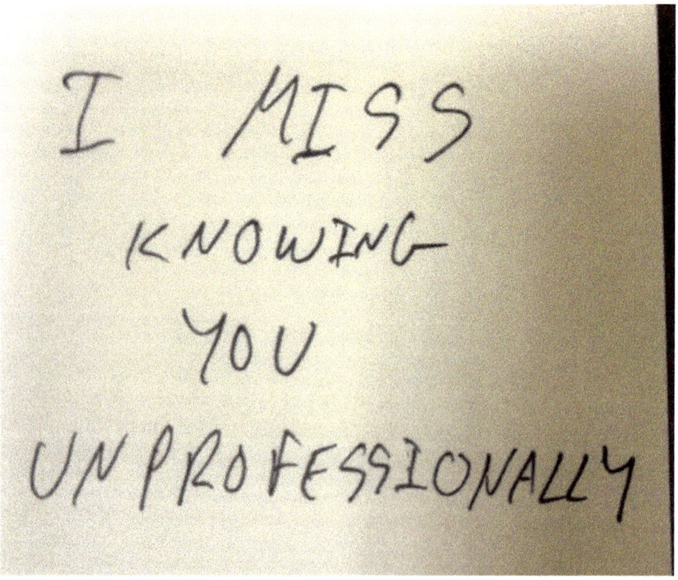
I MISS
KNOWING
YOU
UNPROFESSIONALLY

Another Glass

Pour another glass because I still miss you
Even though many sunsets have passed since I was blindsided
Miserably, I still think about reoccurring throughout the hours
Swimming in Red wine, holding on to hope
Without question your name has been tattooed on my chest plate

I open another bottle, waiting for a distraction
I know that I was only a task
I just wish that I had met you before
At times I get so angry
Because I simply cannot comprehend
Time and currency evidently are not on my side

Must drink this glass slowly, so my head will clear
Dream that the tides are changing, and she will open her eyes!
See that she and I have the chemistry to build upon
Realize this is Nothing that I would stray from
Because her hand is the grasp I hope for
Her package is in the box that I reach for

I've grown tired of drinking these bottles at night
Failed attempts to get my head right
It is difficult to see straight when it's slanted in your favor
Slashes my pride, knowing now that your actions weren't sincere
I know it is emasculating, but I still need you
I know that is pathetic, but I won't believe it's true
I have always wanted someone like you
I hate myself for falling so damn hard for someone

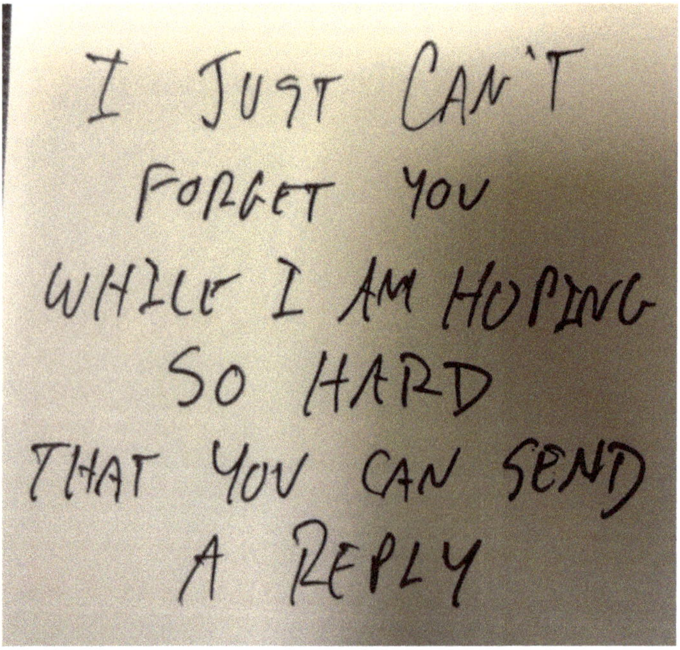
I JUST CAN'T
FORGET YOU
WHILE I AM HOPING
SO HARD
THAT YOU CAN SEND
A REPLY

Apologies

Apologies, my dear
I was unaware of the rules
Coming with a lengthy marriage
I did Not know
That the husband
Was Allowed
To FUCK
A Multitude of women
Involved in a prostitution ring
For a lengthy period of time
Unbeknownst to his partner
Without receiving Any
Kind of consequence
Of ANY Kind
Apologies, my dear
Shiraz is certainly
Seducing me tonight

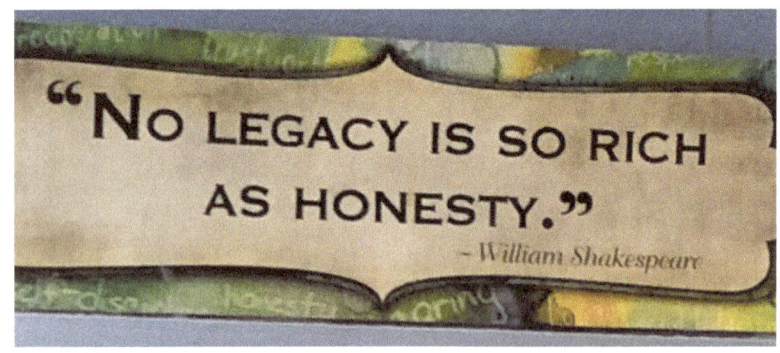

"No legacy is so rich as honesty."

~ William Shakespeare

Attention! Attention!

Need to practice ignoring those who exhibit attention-seeking behaviors
Seeking only to distract from the original infraction committed by the
Exact Same Attention Seeker
That blew up in person AND on social media.
Should have ignored those desperate behaviors from its origin

MY HEARTBEAT QUICKENED
RAPIDLY
SENDING OUT MORSE CODE
TO ALERT THE WORLD
OF MY DESIRE FOR HER.
SHE MOVED ME MORE
EROTO - CHEMICALLY,
MORE THAN ANYONE
I HAD EVER MET.

Certainly

I will not judge you
Or criticize you
You have taken the first step
Toward exiting your Toxic relationship

If only you were able to see
My view when I see you
I can only pray that you wish for more
Certainly, more than current mistreatment
And habitual occasions of infidelity

IT SEEMS AS IF THIS
PAIN WILL NEVER
STOP. I GAVE HER
MY BEST.
I KEEP LOOKIN DOWN,
KNOWIN THAT SHE CHOSE
SOMEONE THAT BROKE HER
IN THE PAST.

Chains

I cannot disagree with your decision to search and find astray
I am still awestruck and honored that your eyes landed upon me
No one will cast blame or question your decision to walk away
You can stay within my walls for solace; you can trust my sincerity

While I may not have the six-figure annual salary of your dreams
You can believe when I say that I will do my damnedest to save you
Along with the world, I think that you are trapped and caged
And I have a feeling that you know this too

We can't run for the future with chains around your ankles
Decisions like these will be those that make or break us

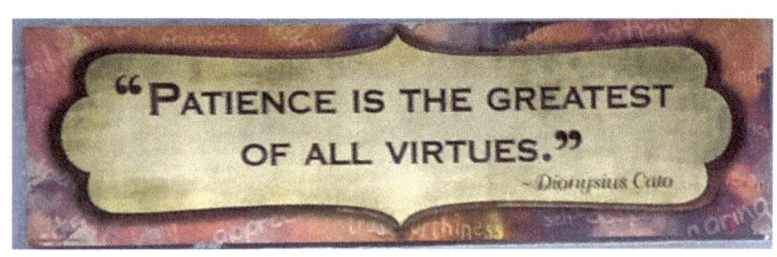

"PATIENCE IS THE GREATEST OF ALL VIRTUES."
– Dionysius Cato

Chasing

Tonight I'm wrapped in my own sheets of shame
Dreams crashed in flames
Time is dull without you

If you could accept my promises, I would find a way to give more
You know that you are shamelessly adored
I can't walk in confidence without you

Embarrassed to say that my shell is cracked
Broken anew
Yet I can't walk away
I'm still chasing after you

Clear

Maybe you didn't want to be saved
I thought that our prior
Triumphs and pains had connected
But maybe you just wanted
To feel desired
To feel wanted
To feel craved for
Enabling you to walk a little taller
Knowing that there was someone
Who wished to receive your attention

IN THAT SHORT TIME
THAT I KNEW YOU

FOR THAT BRIEF TIME
YOU WERE HAPPIER
THAN I HAD EVER SEEN YOU

YOUR STRIDES LANDED
LIGHTER

YOUR SMILE SHINED
BRIGHTER
THAN EVER BEFORE

Comfort

It appears to me
That you are indeed aware that
You Deserve More
You Know there are Countless suitors
Reaching for you
To have and utilize
As you wish

You claimed that you were leaving
You claimed that you were through
You claimed that he could "go Fuck All his hookers!"
You couldn't understand why he brought this pain to you

I Don't Know.
I thought that I understood you.
I thought that you understood me.
I NEVER GAVE A FUCK IF HE WAS HURTING!
You shouldn't have given a Damn either!
I Urge you to let go and leave betrayal behind
I know you say that you can't let go of history

If you want to stay with him
Because of the money
Because of the comfort
I can get that.
It is the only reason
That could make any plausible sense
But if that is indeed the case

You should Not be hurt
Every Next Time he goes astray
The financial comfort of his annual salary
Allows him to do so

Complicated

I offered an escape, opening my pad as safe place, a refuge for you
I will temporarily relocate, providing walls only open to your point of view
Place your sight on my eyes, and you may find it
Place your hand in mine, and we can try it
If you believe in us, we will get through this
When we get through this, you can run with me
Run along the beach, run through the sands
Run until we are soaked with sweat, run until my sweat meets your hands

I can't help feeling and caring for you; I will give my best to carry you
Lift you above me to make you smile; make you giggle to shine like new
Your silhouette can always be found within my mind
Inside of a setting where we will be sharing time
If you believe in us, we will get through this
When we get through this, you will look for me
Look for me on the ground; look for me in the air
Look for me in the water; look for me everywhere

You fit so tight around me; I can be the man you need me to be
I raise my arms and open them wide, inviting you to fly and be set free
There is no doubt that I will give everything to keep you happy
Surely don't need to make this more complicated that it has to be

I LONG TO
HEAR FROM YOU

I WISH THE
CIRCUMSTANCES
WERE DIFFERENT

Constant Thoughts

I try my best Not to miss you;
I may have never even had you?
But just when I think that I am starting to move past you
Just when I think that I am Finally starting to Let Go
Something, Anything, Everything pops up to place your image before me
There is Always Something, Anything, Everything there to remind me of you
Whether it be a song or a sign, a book or a picture, a look or a glance,
Drink or a meal, color or a shade, real or fake, smell or a taste, chair or a dance—
You. Are Always on my Mind.

238

Controlled

Unfortunately,
I believe that you are being controlled.

Allow me to take you by the hand
Allow me to lead you in this dance
You are well aware that you have me
Will you take advantage of this chance?

I hope to keep you in my world
I hope to keep you in my life
I think that I can make you happier
I would allow you to choose for yourself what is right

You may not be able to follow your own mind
Another may have possessive power to influence your life
You should be allowed the freedom to make your own decisions
You deserve to be set free from all your restrictions

Actually,
I believe that you are Quite capable of living within your Own control.

BRAND NEW SUIT PURCHASED
THAT I NEVER GOT TO WEAR
BOUGHT TO DON AT A DINNER
THAT WE NEVER DID SHARE
HANGS IN SORROW AND DESPAIR

Couldn't

I couldn't write the words to open your eyes
I couldn't type the letters to set you free
I couldn't provide the semantics to impress you enough
I couldn't arrange the syntax in my favor to claim you as mine

I have consumed myself with shame and regret
Searching for an uplifting note in the bottom of every bottle
If only time were on my side and banking smiled upon me
Judgement fields of consideration may then be level
But they are not
I have to live with that

OF COURSE
I KNOW THAT HE MAY MAKE
SIGNIFICANTLY MORE MONEY
ANNUALLY THAN I
AND I KNOW THAT
BUT IF YOU STAY IN THIS
ABUSIVE
DYSFUNCTIONAL
UNFAITHFUL RELATIONSHIP
THAT GLOW
THAT SHINE
THAT FIRE
THAT IS SO ADDICTIVE
ABOUT YOU
THAT LIGHT IS GOING TO
FADE AWAY

Decisive

Perhaps, Maybe at another time
I would have been able to hold your hand
The words to make you stay I could not write
Away from your touch I could not withstand

Flipping still frames in my mind
Cherishing our discreet times
Red roses and nipple clips
I can't forget what I could not resist

I felt so damn lost and helpless
Found myself oh, so far below
Your words told me not to persist
Although you unknowingly saved my soul

I reach outstretched to the sky
Scream aloud for wish of you to come
Couldn't speak, just watch as you were turned to fly
Coercion possibly forced our coming undone

This sharp end is so difficult for one to accept
Oh how so swift I was dismissed
Didn't get a chance to speak before you pressed SEND

NOTHING REALLY
MATTERED
I WAS BLINDED
BY YOUR
SMILE

Delusionally,

ALL my writing continues to emerge
-    To you
-    About you
-    Because of you
-    Inspired by you

Embarrassingly,
ALL my writing is *STILL* for you

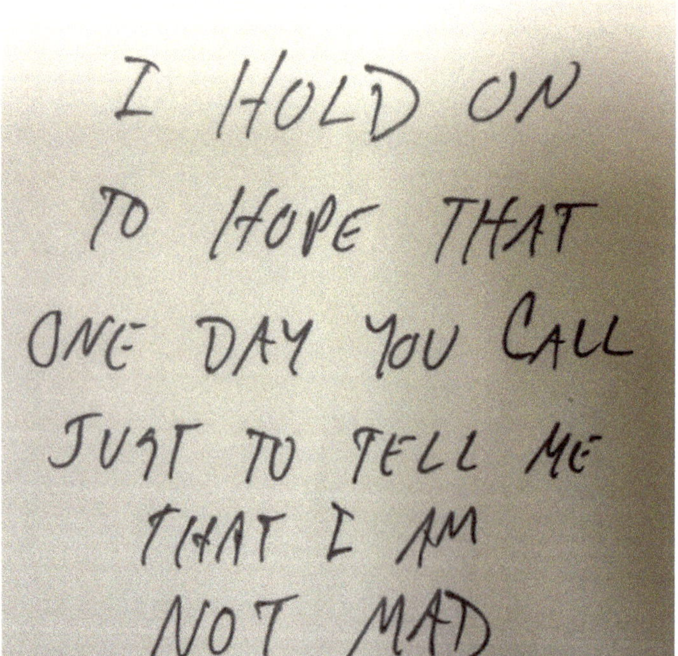
I HOLD ON
TO HOPE THAT
ONE DAY YOU CALL
JUST TO TELL ME
THAT I AM
NOT MAD

Dull

My next few female friends and lovers
May find me Dull
Perhaps a tad bit Boring

I put too much of everything
Into our charade
Excessive lust and immeasurable adoring

Too many words, Too much caffeine,
Too many clamps, Too many flowers,
Too many vibrators, Too many scarves,
Just Too loud, Too many Whiskey sours

Despite the prompt, blunt, unmistakable rejection
I'll wrap my arms around you before asking any questions
I gave all my energy to open your eyes to realize your worth
I Failed to give you sight; I Failed to brighten my world

YOU BURNED ME AS IF
YOUR BEAUTY BORE FLAMES
FROM BENEATH
DESPITE THE SCARS THAT
ONLY I COULD SEE
WHILE YOUR MOUNDS PROVIDED
SERENITY
YOUR LIGHT STILL INSPIRES ME
TO SWIM AND DANCE IN THE SEA
RHYTHM OF THE WAVES
SET ME FREE
TO MOVE AND GLIDE
AWKWARDLY

Edge Of The Cliff

Similar to the population
There are certain things that I dislike about myself
I tend to enjoy/worry/contemplate over things that may never, ever
happen

I worry about Future events
    Future spectacles
    Future scenarios
Just as I trouble myself over losing something/someone that I Never
ever had
She was never even mine
In all likelihood, I became obsessed
She was my everything
She simply Dominated my thoughts
    Demolished my manhood
    Stripped me of my pride
Her ghost tore my body to shreds
Via anxiety/depression/alcoholism/substance abuse

I opened the royal entrance gates for her
Lit the Eucalyptus candles for enchanting light
Laid the rose pedals to guide the way
The anticipation of her footsteps
Has placed the grips of my all-terrain training shoes
Slipping unsteadily on the edge of the cliff

I THOUGHT THAT WE
WERE BOTH BLUE AND
BROKEN
BUT YOU PAINTED MY CHEST
PINK WHILE TITILLATING
MY TENDERNESS WITH
YOUR GRACE, ELEGANCE,
AND ARTISTRY

Even Ida Knows

We were introduced to Ida yesternight
As frightful and destructive as she was
With every Crash
With every Smash
I sat still in darkness, wondering if you were safe
Wondering if you were scared
Wondering if you were terrified
I was wondering if you were all right
I hope that your admirable, lustful confidence was not shaken
By this storm or other unexpected powerful disasters.

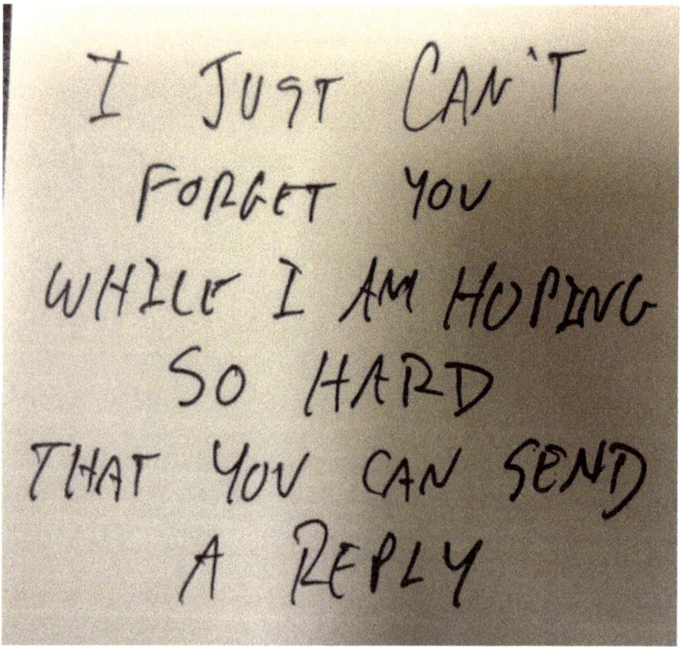
I JUST CAN'T
FORGET YOU
WHILE I AM HOPING
SO HARD
THAT YOU CAN SEND
A REPLY

Every Morning Bell

You are *STILL ALWAYS* on my mind
You seem to have set up a residence in my brain
Your unforeseen silence is antagonizing
This created distance provides anguish
Are those constructed obstacles a personal choice?
Or have those defiant decisions been influenced?
The smile of your silhouette still greets me each morning
The stimulating strides of your ghost glide to my duty station
The wind leads me to reminisce
I can only chuckle at my utter Hopelessness
Accompanied with my protruding Patheticism

WHIMSICAL WONDERS

A Night of
Wicked-tipsy
Ramblings
Influenced by
Honey
Whiskey
And tap water

THE SMELL OF BOOKS

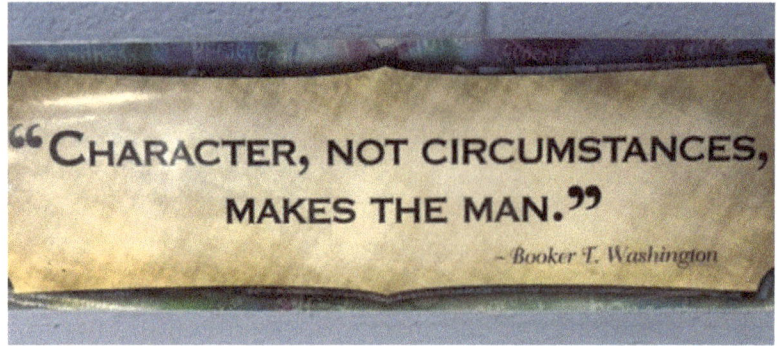

"CHARACTER, NOT CIRCUMSTANCES, MAKES THE MAN."
~ Booker T. Washington

JUST JACK
DREAMING
SIMPLY
TONIGHT
EARS OPEN

MY SMILE WAS SO
MUCH BRIGHTER
MY BLOOD PUMPED SO
MUCH LOUDER
WHEN I KNEW YOU

Dreaming

You habitually excite my loins
More than I could have ever imagined
You perpetually excite my desires
More than I could have ever dreamed

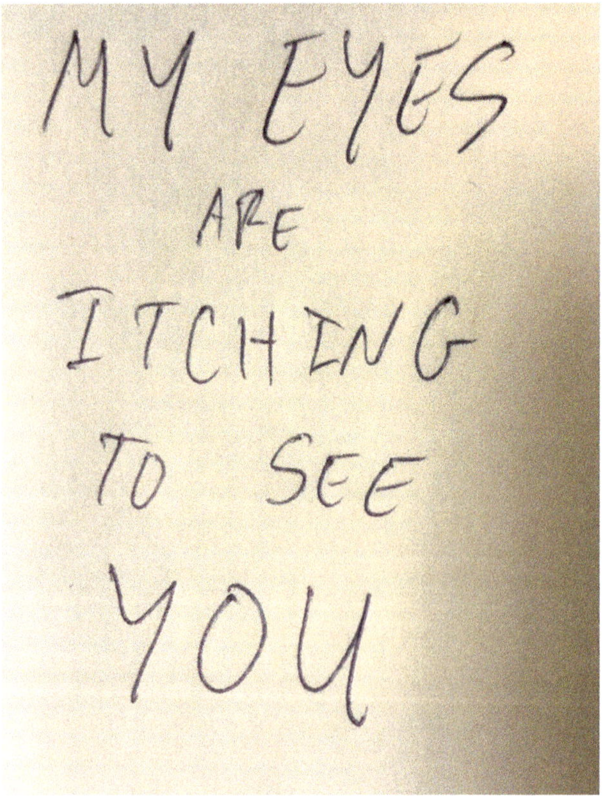
MY EYES
ARE
ITCHING
TO SEE
YOU

Simply

My eyes have been channeled
Toward you all this time
Why couldn't we have crossed paths before?
Still remember first sight of orientation
Did not know I would be so vulnerable
So open, exposing my chest
Giving everything to offer my best

But you turned so suddenly
Throwing wind gusts in the process
To blow me off your back
But now I want you more
As you have become something
I've tasted but cannot have

Reveal the shimmer in your smile to Burn my eyes
Fall into my arms to change my life
While I may not be lucky enough to hold you again
I only wish that I held you longer
Would have been foolish to loosen my grip that much
I Hope these words find you
I Hope these letters feel your touch
I tried to offer you Everything
Everything known and above
Nevertheless, in the End
I simply wasn't Enough

Tonight

Dearest bottle of Honey Whiskey
Warmest clouds surrounding you
I want you there, Loretta Queen,
I'll hope for you tonight

I've sent a sweetest invitation
Slicing myself in two
Feeling as blue as I do, Loretta Queen,
I'll wait for you tonight

Staring at my shape cast by candlelight
Morning alarm reminds of words untrue
Yet hopes anew, Loretta Queen,
I try to say good night

A failed secret fascination
Whispered words through masks to you
Meant next to nothing, Loretta Queen,
I still hope for you tonight

I SEE YOU

EVERYWHERE

MY HUNGER
WILL NEVER BE
SATISFIED.
I WANT
TO EAT
IT ALL

Ears Open

My New companion Jack Daniels
Pointed out to me with laughter
That everything I believed to be real
Everything I believed to be true
Was just a Glorious Fabrication

An Enormous Fucking Lie
That I Foolishly fell for
Because I wanted So Bad
For that Bullshit to be true
Because they were released
from the lovely lips
Of an absolutely Astonishing woman
That I really cared for

I was told Everything I wanted to hear
Everything I needed to hear
When in fact All those whispers
Were Fucking *FALSE*!

I bought them because they came from
Admirably tasty, wine-stained lips
That Never cared for me to begin with
I'M SO Fucked up and Confused.

I just want to communicate with her somehow.
At a time when I know that it is she speaking
Not her property-monitoring, possessive benefactor
Nevertheless, Jack claims he will continue to listen tonight

Just Jack

I need to stop
I find myself hopelessly believing
That this sad secret gets rewritten
So a miracle is permitted
In my favor again
So astronomically arousing
Harmful words have made you feel invisible
When in reality your radiance is blinding
I walk and breathe, unsure what to do
Was Everything I believed just lies?
What can be the sense of this?
Nothing is more painful than this confusion
Here's hope that Jack Daniels understands

I COULDN'T SEE
THE SIGNS
YOUR SORCERY
KEPT ME BLIND

How Could I?

How could I have Not seen this was all on a stage?
How could I have Not seen I was clearly so played?
Ignored all the signs
Chest and Pride made me blind

How could I be so stupid?
Your body out of my league
How could I be so fucking stupid?
Top personality
Intelligent, witty
Generous, funny
How could I be so damn gullible?

Place your hands within mine
Kill me one last time
I cannot forgive myself yet
Have not purified myself yet
Head is still filled with regret
I failed to read the signs
I could not see the light
If your words were right
I foolishly tried to fight
For you I'm so damn dupable

How could I even think that your words were sincere?
How could I even believe you found my body amative?
Why should I have been so confident?
I should have known 'twould end in disappointment

LUSTING
AFTER YOU
WITH SO MUCH
ENTUSIASM —
THE ONLY WAY
I KNEW HOW

How Many?

And WHY am I supposed to care if this Unbelievably Lucky Prick is hurting? This Unfaithful piece of shit deserves excruciating discomfort after all the senseless pain that he has caused you—Multiple times over Multiple years!

You are showing Everyone else by setting the example of How a woman, of your stature nonetheless, should be treated. Am I Seriously supposed to give a Fuck if He is hurting?

Multiple Times! With Multiple Women!

Your letter claimed, "He has been the perfect husband since his last affair."

WWWWWWWWWWWWWHAT THE FFFFUCK!

How many affairs have there been?

How many affairs are acceptable?

How many "experiences" can be bought and still overlooked?

How many affairs will you be able to tolerate?

How can I *NOT* be enough to save you from this?

I WANT YOU
AND THAT HAS NOW
UNRAVELLED THE
END OF
EVERYTHING

I'm Sorry

I know that you may not want to communicate this way
But I Can't Believe those emails were written
Without Heavy outside influence
I Can't Believe that in those April/May/June months prior
You really felt Nothing between us

I know that it can be scary to start over
But you have to realize everything that you are worth

You Should Never have your mind filled with worries of doubt
You Should Never be made to wonder if You Are Enough
I Don't Know How Many Times
On How Many Occasions
A lover should be allowed to receive pleasure from astray
I Don't Know how many times
On How Many Occasions
A lover should be allowed to strike your immaculate face
You may have gotten comfortable with the financial benefits
Of enjoying material things in a material world
As you indeed typed—You may Not be for me
But I never saw you as a "punching bag"-type girl

Despite my open vulnerability
Despite my wounded masculinity

I support you
You can trust me
I will Not do anything to jeopardize what is important to you
I Know that I was Fighting against a thirty-year history
I Know that I may have been waiting for my sinking ship
To arrive at your flying airport in the sky

Just know that I support you
You Deserve to be Happy
You Deserve to be Confident
You Deserve to be Secure
You Deserve to receive Loyalty

If you need me for something
If you need me for anything
I will be there for you

XXX-XXXX

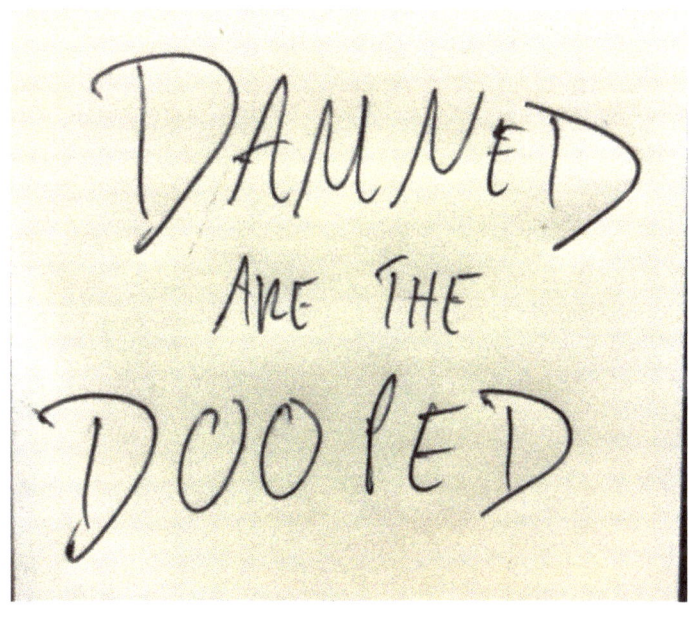

I HAVE TO WONDER.....
HOW AM I VIEWED
THROUGH YOUR
ALMOND EYES

Into The Unknown

Unfortunately, I believe that I have Feverishly fallen
For an astonishing woman
Unable to display the bravery
Required when leaping out of one's comfort zone
And landing into the unknown

SOFT SUPERMARKET BEAUTY
SENT IN STILL FRAME HOLDING
WARM, GENTLE HANDS
CUPPING BOTTLE OF YELLOW TAIL

FINE, FINISHED FINGERNAILS
CONTRASTING TINTED GLASS OF
SEDUCTIVE SHIRAZ
HYPNOTIZING HANDS
MESMERIZING MAROON

Just A Touch

I have brought upon myself all this sorrow
I have brought upon myself all this pain
I simply hoped for one time to take you walking
I have not yet gotten to walk with you
Cherishing and Holding your Angel Hands

I guess that I never wanted to be just an undercover lover
I wanted to be admired and referred to as your boyfriend
But I was Not Enough to Save you from another
Just a Fool Not to Realize that this Fantasy would end

I understand that things may be comfortable
I know that people can be afraid of change
Sometimes we must Free ourselves to get what we Deserve
Sometimes we must Free ourselves to see what we are Worth

I know that I can make you Happy
But I Can't Force you to take that chance
Only hope that you agree to take a Walk with me
While I'm Cherishing and Holding your Angel Hands

I STILL SEE YOU
EVERYWHERE UPON
THESE BLUE GROUNDS
THE SLEEK STRIDES
OF YOUR SILHOUETTE
CAUSES THE ZIPPER
OF MY PANTS TO
PULSATE

Just Important

Aside from the mesmerizing body
Your intellect is equally as intriguing
You are well aware that a man who truly cares for you
Will give you absolutely No reason to doubt his loyalty or devotion

He will Never take you for granted.

A just man will keep you above and beyond anything and everything

He would fight for you and Not with you. Would Not strike you hard (even if you slap him first).

He would remember your likes and dislikes. He would remember that you have a taste for cappuccino (more creamer and sugar than espresso)

He understands what is important to you

IN A WORLD WHERE COMMUNICATION
    WAS TEED WITH LIMITS
I USED MY PEN AS A WEAPON
    FILLED WITH TIMELESS INK
I SCREAMED AND SHOUTED
    UNTIL MY THROAT WAS STRICKEN

I HAVE MEANT EVERY SINGLE WORD
    THAT I HAVE WRITTEN

Just Like That

Just like that
When you pressed SEND
Your enchanting photos could No Longer
Be developed for my sight
Your voice will No Longer
Narrate my fantasy
That I could No Longer allow myself to dream about

When I read those typed words
You became a memory that I will No Longer
Be possible to relive
Your almond eyes can No Longer
Make me hungry with carnal desire
Your savory curves can No Longer
Produce an overabundance of saliva in my mouth

After reading the last word of that painful email
You became a landmark I could No Longer visit
You became a melody I could No Longer listen to
You possessed the hand that I could No Longer try to hold
The story of Us simply can No Longer wished be told

Instantly and Timelessly
You became Everything
I only wish I had

SEEMS TO BE
ENDLESS TIME
YOUR SEDUCTIVE SILHOUETTE
SEEMS TO FANTASTICALLY FLY
AROUND MY HEAD
LIKE A SATELLITE

Just Promise Me

That you do not believe that this
Subpar, Abusive, Toxic love
In which you Willingly remain
Is the Most True and Best Love
That is available for you to receive.

JUST PROMISE ME

STILL

WHEN I SET SIGHTS
ON YOUR SILHOUETTE
RISING SOUNDS OF THE
QUICKENG PULSE AND
THUNDEROUS CRESCENDO
IN MY TROUSERS
CAN BE HEARD BY
THE MASSES

Known

Despite this newfound vocabulary
Which certainly has been birthed under the influence of another
The world believes that you find yourself uneasy
Because even you know
That you were meant for so much more than this
Your powerful and determined words before summer break enlightened eyes that cannot close
You must stop holding yourself constrained to let yourself fly

You know that you are Too mesmerizing, Too astonishing, Too remarkable, Too valuable
To be with a man who has proven multiple times, on multiple occasions
That he simply cannot understand your beauty
His weight is holding you back and closing your wings
Not everyone can respect everything that you are worth

Your masses are Shocked by your mind
And Stunned by your Almond eyes
Nostrils are pleased by your Lavender scent
Well aware that you walk too rare for average compliments
We are paralyzed when your freckles lift as you smile
Warm in the waist when your maroon lips shine
Bulldozed below the waist when your laughter can be heard
Looking through the public eye—you deserve the world

AN ADULT CONVERSATION IS NOT EQUIVALENT TO INTERCOURSE

Lack Of Photographs

I don't even have a picture of us together
Nothing to remember the time we shared
We have no evidence that I was ever by your side
I had to delete everything you sent to me
Just so I could begin to try to forget you
Unsuccessfully
I Failed
You glanced my way
Only in my memory
Your body
Your mind
Your laugh
Your bottom
Your giggle
Your breasts
Your eyes
Your pedals
Your loyalty
Your snort
Your resilience
You shared these things with me
Only in my memory

I HOPE THESE WORDS
FIND YOU WELL
IT HAS TAKEN ME SOME TIME
TO SIT AND SPELL
EVERYTHING THAT I TRY TO SAY
BUT I KNOW THAT I MUST BE
READY TO CONVEY

Malbec

I was speaking with Malbec earlier
And he posed an interesting point:

You entered my world as a *Dream*
Before I laid eyes upon you
And began feverishly fondling myself

When you made yourself available
That fantasy became a *Reality*
Until I was forced to Stop fooling myself

Your silhouette now reminds me
Of your preference to become a *Memory*
Images permitted only to be revisited when touching myself

THERE IS ONLY
ONE VOICE
I WANT TO HEAR
NOTHING
HAS EVER BEEN
THIS CLEAR

Moments

I am beginning
To feel that you may just
Believe that we shared
A few moments
A few pictures
A few kisses
A few touches—
But those moments
Changed everything
For me moving forward

AS IF I WERE
UNABLE TO FUND
OUR FANTASY
I WAS CAST ASIDE
AS INADEQUATE

Muse

My heart longs for you
My heart has always longed for the promise of you
My chest continues to pound for you as my muse
Most places in which you had No idea
Maybe No intention to ever touch
You moved my essence in feelings that I didn't even know I felt

You have given me drive
You have given me purpose
You have given me inspiration
Everything that I write
Every word is all for you, Loretta

MY WICKED-TIPSY MIND
IS SOAKED IN PAIN
CAN'T HEAR A THING BUT
SOUND OF BROKEN BOTTLES
AND HEARTS TO WISHES
THAT I CAN'T IGNORE
IN A WORLD WHERE I HAVE
NO CONTROL I GRASP ON TO
HOPE THAT I WANT TO HOLD

Name

You seem to seduce my mind everywhere
I seem to search for your face in everything
In this desolate solitude of Cabernet
I think of you
Your smile
Your bottom
Your breasts
Your bare pedals
Running swiftly through the saltwater sands
You possess my zipper
You own my chest
You are the one I think of
When I awaken in the middle of the night
You are the one of whom I toss and turn
Until my morning alarm sounds
You are the one I fantasized of
Before I even knew your name

I CAN UNDERSTAND IF
YOU'RE NOT SOUND ENOUGH
TO WRITE
I CAN UNDERSTAND IF
YOU'RE UNABLE TO STRAY FROM
THE GREEN
I'VE BEEN RUNNING IN CIRCLES
FOR SOME TIME HOPING FOR RESPONSE
EVERY STEP LANDS LOST AS I
CAN'T FIND THE WORDS TO SAY

Natural Disaster

Ida was a Monstrous storm to say the least
My residence has been deemed unlivable
My pickup truck has sustained significant scratches, dents with a
black eye
Due to recklessly destructive flying sheet metal.
I haven't spoken with you since the lone phone call
Following your rejuvenating Arizona crusade.
I hope that you are safe;
I hope that you had a chance to evacuate.
I want the damage received to your property to be minimal.
I want to see and speak with you again.
I need to see you again.

I LET MYSELF GO

I LET MYSELF FALL

I LET MYSELF FEEL

Neverending

He may have loved you at one time in the past
When he may have treated you appropriately
But his financial salary has opened his options
Believing that his income guarantees forgiveness
For any unfaithful actions committed without any consequence
Even if, somehow, he is reborn and rejuvenated
And he finally realizes how attractive you appear
Only temporarily for a few sunsets before he is led astray
He couldn't possibly appreciate how fucking sexy
And radiant you are to me in Merely a few moments
Just in case you have foolishly forgotten
Your feet are constantly dancing and prancing
Within my every dream and never-ending thought

I SEE YOU

YOU KNOW YOU ARE MISTREATED
YOU KNOW YOU DESERVE MORE
UNFORTUNATELY YOU CANNOT
LEAVE THE LUXURY

No Explanations

I can't explain it
But this time
I cannot move past the girl that crushed me
I can't explain it
But this time
I was discarded for one that has previously hurt her
Multiple Times
With Multiple Women
On Multiple Occasions
I was confused how one that made her devastated could be chosen above me
I can't explain it
This time I gave open truths
This time I gave my complete self
This time I may have given too much
This time I Certainly cared too much
I am shunned wearing pain, yet I only want to embrace her
I can't explain it
I will take every measure to increase my chances
I will take every measure in hopes that she reads these words
I will take every measure to hold on to everything she left behind
I will take every measure to keep the things that made her laugh
I can't explain it
But I have to hold on to this bowling pin
I can't explain it
But I can't let go of these memories of Loretta

YOU HAVE OCEANS
OF TIME
TO MOVE PAST THE PAIN THAT
HE HAS CAUSED
YOU HOLD THE CLOCK
TO SEEK SMILES
BORN FROM SOMEONE ELSE
NO RUSH
TAKE ALL THE TIME YOU NEED

No Longer

I no longer have any plans or schemes
I no longer have any hopes or dreams
I no longer have anything of importance
As I no longer have you

I no longer share any pics of my private fire
I no longer receive any pics of pads that I desire
I no longer have anything of importance
As I no longer have you

I had happiness then bewilderedness
Causing a swirling shock, indeed how we progressed
Since you chose a repeatedly unfaithful over me
Your decision quickly brought upon misery
In which I have found myself so engulfed since

I no longer have these feelings to share
I no longer have exciting pics of a current love affair
It appears I no longer have anything at all
As I no longer have you
But maybe, just maybe, I never really had anything to begin with?

THIS SILENCE.
YOUR SILENCE.
PAINFUL.
HAVE I GONE DEAF?
AM I STILL TRYING
   TO VALIDATE?
DEPLORABLE.

Not That Dude

I don't want to be the dude
That looks back regretfully
Thinking that I could have been Awesome
Thinking that I could have had the girl of my dreams
But I was too damn scared to do anything about it
No.
Not now.
I will Not walk away
I want the satisfaction of knowing that I tried my Best
I wish for the confidence that comes with having her by my side

PLEASE STOP FIGHTING

FOR AFFECTION
AND APPROVAL
FROM THE UNGRATEFUL

Obvious

As far as my blatant, emasculating advances,
If they have been rejected that is fine
I can learn to live with that
However, I don't believe that I have done anything to be
Disrespected, Insulted, and Mocked Numerous times
Written in your sent emails of rejection

I know that you did not write those words alone
You are Too Kind;
You are Too Gentle;
You are Too Compassionate;
You are Too Sympathetic
I know that you would not write the words to bring Blunt, Direct
pain intentionally (without aid)
You have always treated others the same way in which you would like
to be treated by them
You are Too Wonderful

You comically saw the need to CC your Overseer
Verifying for his approval of the offensive wording that was sent in
your Dismissal Address

Contrary to your charming features
There is something unattractive about a woman who repeatedly
undervalues her self-worth
There is something sour about a lady who forgives and returns to a
repetitively unfaithful
Try to comprehend your exquisite value; You are Better than This

You are Too Hypnotic to misunderstand your Powers
You certainly will come across numerous admirers

You will have suitors who claim that they want to be with you
And those admirers who actually care and feel for you
Without a doubt
You are Too Wise and Too Capable
To confuse my heartfelt actions with his meaningless words

I SAW HOW LOYAL
AND DEVOTED YOU CAN BE
TO YOUR PARTNER.
THAT IS WHAT I WANTED.
I DO NOT KNOW
HOW ANYONE COULD JEOPARDIZE
THE TREASURE
THAT IS LORETTA

On Cliff's Edge

Certainly, displayed by those begging for attention
And also seen in my Painfully Pathetic Writing as of late
There can be found NO More Desperate and Shameless a man
Than a hopeless romantic on the edge
Of losing the woman that possesses his Timeless affection

SO MUCH MORE
I WANTED TO DO WITH
YOU
SO MUCH MORE
I WANTED TO TASTE OF
YOU
SO MUCH MORE.......

Only You

You are the only person I think of when I walk before a library.
You are the only person I think of when I am jogging on the beach
in aqua socks.

We never got to run together.

I wish that you were with me.
I wish that you could be beside me.
I wish that you could be here.

I have so many words that I would like to say to you.
I have so many acts that I wish to perform upon you.
I have so many questions I hope that you can answer.

I WANTED US
SO BAD
I WAS BLIND

Plea

Greetings, gorgeous—

Hopefully your surroundings have been becoming more pleasant within your atmosphere as of late?

I have been thinking about you and the well-being of your children ridiculously often, sweetheart.

While it may be out of our control,

Having email as our only means of communication has proven to be

An incredibly taxing task to say the least.

I know that you are going through extremely difficult circumstances right now,

But I only want what is best for you Loretta.

You know how I feel about everything that you deserve,

Even if it does not involve a teacher,

It is clear that you are worthy of more.

I am in too deep and will not be able to rest easy

Unless I know that you will be treated properly—

Unless I know that you are taken care of—

Unless I know that you will be all right.

Naturally, of course, I hope that you feel I have a part in what you feel is best for you.

It is easy to understand that you need space right now.

Hopefully I hear from you soon

STEPS WERE LANDING IN DARKNESS
TILL A SHIMMERING SMILE
CAME FROM YOU
SHAMEFUL WHAT HOPE WILL LEAD
GULLIBLE PEOPLE TO
I NEVER IMAGINED THAT I WOULD
HAVE A CHANCE TO BE WITH YOU

I NEVER IMAGINED THAT IT WOULD
HURT LIKE THIS
WHEN I LOST YOU

Power Of The Beholder

Your confidence required rebuilding, so I sent you a pic of my pride
As I was grasped by your electric eccentricities decorative for sight
I found myself falling in too deep in such a short time
Falling farther into darkness I'm reaching back for light
I thought that our stories connected, experiences intertwined
Looked forward to feathers tickling as my hands were tied
Clamps precisely placed upon your breasts to enhance your smile
Your scarf to be tied around my head in order to keep me blind
Do you ever/Did you ever think of me?
Constant thoughts of you still seem to resonate
Do you ever/Did you ever think of me?
Against wishes, honest truths can be tough to take
Could I have possibly been kept in the dark?
Was this Really ALL just pretend?
Did I seriously allow myself to be left in the dark?
Was I pushed aside as irrelevant before this even began?
We shared our heartbreaks of the past
Prepped ourselves to push them aside and fall fast
Wondering, we fell so quickly could this last?
Of All this I can make No Sense
I can only plead ignorance
While a simple, but reliable defense
My head is spinning rapidly into infinity
I Refuse to try to understand this story
What if I told you that I was not like the others before?
What if I told you that I was not a work to be placed on one of your
bookshelves?
Oh, Lovely Loretta, you are the Beholder
You possess the Power to see ALL that will and will NOT falter

WHEN YOUR BENEFACTOR
NO LONGER LOOKS YOUR WAY
AS YOUR FOREMAN OVERSEER
HAS NO KIND WORDS TO SAY
JUST KNOW THAT MY VOICE WILL COME
I'LL BE THERE WHEN YOU HAVE NO ONE
YOU DON'T HAVE TO WALK ALONE
PLACE YOUR HAND IN MINE
CRY TO ME

Problematic Issues

The problematic issue is that
With the confiscation of cell phones
And reprimanding of social media accounts
Along with the Property monitoring of email accounts
I Don't Know with whom I'm speaking
The multiple personality/schizophrenia behaviors
Seem to be displayed through each media outlet
I have Not laid eyes on you—
Or given any reason for such an Immediate
Cease and Dismiss—
Since escorting you to your ride
For your appealing hair appointment
Before your departure for Arizona,
I trust you appeared remarkable.

YOU ARE ENTHRALLING
YOU ARE AMAZING
YOU ARE ASTOUNDING
HE DESPERATELY FLIPPED OUT
BECAUSE HE COULD NOT
CONTROL YOU FOR A WHILE
BUT I KNOW I CAN'T SAVE YOU
ONLY YOU CAN DO THAT

Reminders

Before we crossed paths
I waltzed through days
Hoping for a partner like you
Searching through the masses
For your divine face
You stole my breath with your almond eyes
When you chose to glance my way
And titillatingly tease with a shot of your underboob
You snatched my everything
With your charming charisma
Thus, you still dwell comfortably within
The quiet pauses between my thoughts

I understand that you were Never mine to lose
But it still hurts as if I lost you all the same
To maintain a social smile, I occasionally giggle
Pondering if I actually meant something to you?

But there seems to be No Escape
In the Lustrous Lands of Loretta
The Entire Imaginable Universe seems
To be painted with pictures of you

I STILL LOSE SLEEP
HOW COULD YOU CHOOSE A
  REPEATEDLY UNFAITHFUL
PHYSICAL ABUSER OVER ME?
  YOUR LEGS MAY FEEL CHAINED
TO KEEP YOU BESIDE POSSESSOR
  BUT YOU MY DEAR
    HOLD THE KEY
ALLOW YOURSELF TO RUN FREE

Saved

Each time you took a step toward me
Each time you took my breath away
I wanted to hold you close
But we couldn't manage to keep our secret safe.
No one else has ever so moved me
No one else has ever received pictures of my pride
I had never before felt comfortable enough—
That natural feeling made me want to stay.

Your image put the worst behind me
Every time I placed my sight on you
Your voice seemed to lighten my face.
Out of all my fanciful illusions
I so wanted this dream to come true.
My steps before only led me to be lost
Now found with arms around you in my place.

Allow me to land my strides toward you
Allow me to feel your palms within my hands.
Without question I have crossed the line
I just want to take you wherever this may lead.
There is a yearning deep inside of me
I am confident that we will both find joy.
This feeling is yelling from within
To just let this urge be free.

But I have found myself in a drunken nightmare—
Anxious? Nervous? Paranoid? Yet too buzzed to care.
Each and every countless glass is filled with wine
I am left outside of your picture frame, waiting for my time.

Out of all those upsetting mistakes
Out of all those actions committed out of spite
Just award me to be yours
I would give anything to make you mine.

Unfortunately, it matters not what you do or say
These feelings cannot subside quietly anyway.
Efforts of such extents have me dying to see you
Yet through this all—you make me feel so alive.

If you told me that you wanted more
If you stretched out your hand for me
I would sprint through all this chaos
To wrap my arms around you to hold beside me.

I have lived through many failures
Been rejected on many occasions throughout my life.
My eyes have always searched for the hope of you.
As your tears have now dried from my shoulder
Let me know, Loretta—
Was I enough to save you?

I want you to know that you Saved me.
I will certainly fight for you
But I don't want to fight over you
Just know that you Saved me—it's True.

SINCE 1ST SHARED BNB LESSON
ON YOUR LIBRARY STAGE
YOU BUILT A BEATING BULGE
BEARING YOUR NAME IN MY BOXERS
YOUR CUNNING CHARISMA
YOUR KILLER CURVES
YOUR CARESSABLE CHARACTER
HOW COULD YOU NOT BE CHERISHED?

Say Anything

The last Email she sent Killed me
No Way could she have written those words
The message contained the Exact Opposite
Of everything she had been whispering to me
The Exact Opposite of choreography
Displayed in her seduction dance for me

But Never Before had I read words so devastating:
"Please don't try to contact me anymore."

But I CANNOT back away
Now I *CANNOT* leave it like this

I dropped and slammed my pride
Via text messages and photos
In what seems too long ago

This was a different shade of hurt
This had a different kind of bleeding
I won't turn away without saying something
I can't turn away without saying anything

Self

Self-Deprecating
I feel as if all of my efforts
Everything I gave was still not enough
Everything I gave could not live up
I gave it all Driven by my chest
I tried to separate myself from the rest
I hoped she would notice the pleasantries I placed within her world
Not merely report a constant flowing of flattering words
I followed my pursuit of her into an attractive, chaotic forest
Running after her tested my sanity throughout the process
I desired to be engulfed within her completely
Similar to shots taken down her throat quickly
Providing warmth and satisfaction like her whiskey
I needed everything she possessed
I offered her to Enjoy and Own my best
Self-Mutilating

Suddenly

Even with this distance
You have constructed between us
You have suddenly become
Everything that I care about
I feverishly feel something
Pulling me toward you
Some Force dragging me
Your gravitational pull tugging me
Toward You
Inexplicably
You don't see your reflection as I do
View yourself as the world does
This silence built with these barriers
Hurts more than any truthful words
You could say
I need to hear something from you
I need to hear anything from you
Through this pain
I have dropped my shame
You are worth it all

Things Happen

The darnedest things happen when I drink alone
I drink Shiraz—and I think of you and I fall
I drink Cabernet—and I think of you and I trip
I drink whiskey—and I think of you and I ache
With each sip I think of you, and I drown
With each belch I think of you
And I realize that I failed

Unanimous

I have been told before
That I was sneaky like a thief
Making it possible to take Anything
That I wished to have near me
Evidently, as of late
This statement has been proven untrue
I was unable to steal you away
Rescuing you from a toxic relationship
    You were meant to be respected
    You were supposed to be admired
    You were built to be cared for
    You were designed to be worshipped
Do Not let some Asshole make
You Foolishly believe otherwise
Believe Me when I tell you it is Not true
Believe Me when I tell you one to say so is a Fool
Believe Me when I tell you that could Not be more Inaccurate
Believe Me when I tell you the World is in Agreement

Unanswered

I know that you
Will likely hurt me
(Hard to leap from comfort
To the unknown)
But if you could
Please give me a response.
Living with Rejection
Is painful
But it is so much better
Than dying with
Unanswered questions

Unforgettable

Jogging on the beach with aqua socks on my feet
While landing every sinking step, I thought of you
All the pain I felt came straight from me
Can't place any blame—I drowned myself within you
Gave you my shoulder when you saw your lover's true attitude

Countless images of you reside within my head
I made you smile when your almond eyes were filled with tears
I would give you every word, but enough could not be said
To rest your chest against mine with toned arms wrapped around me

I am always reminded of the grounds upon which we walked
With my every passing before the doors withholding your collection
of books
Still get chubby entering your office where our lips first locked
Still finding myself lost in the silhouette of hypnotizing, enhanced
looks

I wish that we could share countless more times
But that is outside of the arrangement that you made
Wounded pride and a shattered chest were the prices I paid
To be an ignorant, fortunate chosen Revenge contract-hire

Jogging on the beach with aqua socks on my feet
Every sinking step rejuvenates dreams of you
Seems nothing will take away this fantasy
You will always be my wish of more dreams coming true

I cannot forget this past spring
Sharing pic for pic

Erotica notes and images
Sent fearlessly by text

Scenes continue to haunt me through days and sleepless nights
Hanging on to a thread of hope, I cannot put this to rest
Emasculating and humiliating do not misconstrue
No matter what I do
I cannot forget you

Unintended Plans

It wasn't in the plans
It was Never on the agenda
You were Never supposed to mean this much to me
I was Never supposed to Fall this Hard.
Unfortunately,
I fell harder, with Marvelous speed, than I ever imagined I would fall for someone
This shameful desire for you keeps me holding on to transparent hope
Because it hurts more than anything before
To let go of this dream

V And W

Shiraz has confirmed
That I can provide you
With essentials to make you happy
Loyalty, Respect, Passion, and Understanding
Exercising Patience
I believe there is Still time
For you to comprehend your
Own Value and Worth

Wants

There are others who want me
But I still want you
Mechanically I entertain them
But I still want you
And you want someone else
You are likely reconciling
Moving on
Making things work
I can't begin to understand why
But I Still want you

Wind Gusts

Her wind gusts were forceful and terrorizing
I stepped outside to feel her power of Hurricane 150+ mph
To take my mind away from the lingering pain
The flying sheet metal screaming and screeching around
The scraps Yelled, "Danger!" and caused Immediate Destruction
The strong winds clashed against my sturdy stance Violently
Similar with the Misty Bayou sound structure
I miss what I only thought we had

Spirit

On my first air flight since
The orchestrated abrupt cutoff
And SPIRITually
ALL I can see throughout this cabin
Are visions of the photo you sent
Visions of You and your daughter
Pictured in matching face masks
For safety and protection of others
Masks are still required aboard the plane
Placing your luscious figure upon
Many, Numerous Caucasian women
As this Loretta-posing woman placed
In a seat of the row before me
Orders a Seagram's 7 'n 7
I allow myself to smile
While pondering numbers of
Airline Whiskey bottles you could take down
When aboard a flight to Baltimore?
Even sixty-five thousand feet in the air
Despite myself
Dreams of you can still
Lift me Up
Even though I understand
I can't let go
I hope you are happy
I wish you are well

Almond Strike

You walked with Everything Magical
That I previously believed to be
Out of my league
Aside from my countless dreams
Featuring your Astonishing lure
My admiring gazes in your direction
The complimentary words I spoke with you
My flattering actions toward you
My lustful photos and texts sent to you
They ALL reflect the Obvious—
I have been yours ever since
You struck me with your almond eyes
I feel as if I have to Fight
Now that I have tasted this Fairy Tale

Franzia

Tossing and Turning under my sheets again
Your face imprinted on back of my eyelids
Bottles of wine can't help me sleep
Just curls my brow while wondering what I did

Speaking soft words with your silhouette
Keeps me awake until 4:00 AM
Asking—How could you look past prostitutes?
Why keep running back to him?

I just sucker punched this cardboard box
Of Franzia Delicious Red Wine
I twist myself Foolish and Run myself Mad
As I can't seem to remove you from my mind

My Drive won't let me shake your memory
Your grip hold is Divine
Tearing myself up over how far to extend
My hand just to reach you one more time
Unsure if you want to cross paths
Certainly Not receiving the signs
Substance abuse and alcohol can't assist
Excessive amounts aren't enough to stray you from my mind

IT FRIGHTENS
THE FUCK OUT OF ME
THAT I WON'T HEAR YOUR
VOICE AGAIN
AND MY DRIVE WILL NOT
BE FUELED TO MOVE ME
THE WAY THAT I WAS
WHEN I WAS WITH YOU

CAN'T GET YOUR TASTE
OUT OF MY MOUTH
MY LOVELIEST LICK
CARNIVOROUS KISS
FINESSING FUCK
THERE IS NO RETURN FOR ME
ADDICTED TO YOUR FALSE INNOCENCE
YOU ARE INCOMPARABLE

IF THAT IS REALLY WHERE
YOU ARE SUPPOSED TO BE —
WHY DO YOU SPEND SLEEPLESS
NIGHTS OVERTHINKING?
IF IT WERE TRUE — WHY
DO YOU FEEL PAIN AND UNREST?
THIS IS NOT HAPPINESS
THIS CONSTANT BATTLE IS
NOT LOVE

YOU DESERVE SO MUCH MORE

UNDERSTAND — YOU ARE
NOT REPLACEABLE
YOU LEFT AN IMPRESSION
UPON MY SOUL —
I WILL ALWAYS REMEMBER YOU
THE FIRST TIME WE SPOKE
THE LAST TIME WE TOUCHED
AND ALL MOVEMENTS IN BETWEEN
YOU ARE IRREPLACEABLE
YOU ARE SIGNIFICANT

PLEASE
DO NOT ALLOW
YOUR LOYALTY
TO TRANSFORM TO
SLAVERY
SWEETHEART.

AS I DEVALUE MYSELF
POUR MY EVERYTHING
ON TO PAPER
LORETTA
WILL YOU SEND A REPLY?
WILL YOU SAY MY NAME?
WILL I HEAR YOUR VOICE?

LORETTA, YOU ARE THE
LOVELIEST
MOST RAVISHING
TENDEREST
MOST ASTONISHING
WOMAN I HAVE EVER KNOWN
- AND EVEN THAT DOESN'T SAY
ENOUGH.

Epilogue

It kills me to mentally picture
You hanging on the arm of the unfaithful
Undeserving of Everything that you are
Enjoying the benefit of your companionship
Exclusively due to the financial comfort
Nonetheless, a hurtful lesson has been learned
Holding painfully true in these modern times

Nothing is Done
Until it is Done
Nothing is Final
Until it is Final

Nevertheless
I am Still Standing Here
I Must Convince Myself
To Become a Man of Stone

Thank you for your time and all your efforts put forth

About the Author

Steve Stone is a secondary-education English instructor in a reputable school attended by the general public. Holding a master's degree in education, along with a bachelor's degree in performing arts, he enjoys the dramas and tragedies in motion on a stage. He enjoys the literature of Shakespeare and William Wordsworth, while being moved by the British Romantics.

Stone was never so struck until he came across the words surrounding the librarian at his educational institute. Her loyalty, devotion, and charisma—along with her stunning physical figure—blinded him as simply incomparable. When her eyes glanced his way, following repetitive actions from her unfaithful husband, Stone merely thought he held the world in his hands. Presently, he runs neighborhood streets and grounds, searching for what he once held.

Lightning Source UK Ltd.
Milton Keynes UK
UKHW051341281122
412966UK00011B/116